# DUNGEON MOTHER

BY

**LADY HILLARY**

# DEDICATION

*This book is dedicated to Sir Robert, my Knight in Shining Armor, and to my Lady Laura, who changed my life forever with her love and kindness.*

# ACKNOWLEDGMENT

*Chardonnay, who always loved me just the way I am.*

*Mistress Georgia, for her guidance and encouragement in writing this book*

# PROLOGUE

I write this book to honor a promise to my granddaughter, Chardonnay, to document my story. It is my love letter to BDSM, which gave me so much over the forty-two years I worked professionally in that special and unique world. Everything I write is based solely on my experiences and my perceptions.

Professional kink wrapped its arms around me and told me I was safe, I was beautiful, I was smart, and I was loved. It brought me inner peace. It is impossible to explain to someone who is not into the scene or has never experienced it. BDSM gave me balance. It filled a physiological need in me. When I began, I was a masochist, and each time I played with a real Master who knew what he was doing, it was extremely cathartic for me. It was such a release, both mentally and physically, that I started to feel more balanced in my life. BDSM afforded me so many opportunities for inner growth and financial stability, which, as a single mother of three, was especially important.

I was so blessed to be able to join the community when it was underground at a time when most of the people involved were truly into BDSM and not just there for kicks. Everyone took pride in what they were doing and the atmosphere Because even when you were submissive, it could be a very loving and nurturing experience. It was a school of hard knocks, and I had to learn my lessons quickly, but the people around me looked after me and showed me the ropes.

I was a doormat when I began, with absolutely no self-esteem.

But the women I worked with over the years encouraged me and made me understand that I deserved better. They made me understand that I did not deserve to be beaten black and blue by everyone who sessioned with me and how my submission was a gift that should only be shared with those deserving of it.

It was challenging to navigate the double life I was leading because, as sex workers in the '90s, we all had to hide what we did for a living from the outside world. It was impossible to do the simplest things, like rent an apartment, open a bank account, or even just have a conversation with someone you just met, because you had to lie all the time. There was always the danger of losing your children, which I unfortunately saw happen to many dear friends and colleagues in my early years. If someone became upset with you, that would be the first thing they would threaten you with. They were going to report you, and you were going to lose your kids. That made going into any new situation incredibly stressful for me. I surrounded myself with my chosen family and protected my kids at all costs. Luckily, I managed to shelter them from knowing what I actually did for a living until they were well into their teens.

Most of the women I met over the years were bright and beautiful human beings who happened to be kinky and were lucky enough to be able to make a living doing it. I do pray that one day, sex workers will be afforded all the benefits of any other worker and not be shamed for what we do.

Kink had been my passion in life before I even knew what it was. It was always there, and it still is. I feel blessed that life led me

to the path I chose and that I was lucky enough to live out my fantasies, work out things my shrinks never could, and grow to become a positive force in the community that empowered other women. I gave women the choice to call the shots in their sessions and free them from the exploitation I suffered in my earlier years in the professional world of kink. Kink changed my life, and it saved my life.

I thank all those who came before me and paved the way so I could feel free to be who I am.

# DEBBIE

*Debbie six years old*

*I am twelve years old and sitting in a psychologist's office. I am alone and don't really know why I am here, and all I feel is fear. The room is sterile and cold, with one of the windows open, creating a breeze strong enough to make the blinds hit the metal on the windows on each return: clank, clank, clank. There are college degrees hanging in cheap frames on the wall and a bookcase with an assortment of colorful children's toys in boxes. Why am I alone in this room? After what seems an eternity, the door opens, and a man enters the room alone. He is wearing glasses and has dark hair. I do not want to look at his face. He feels as cold as the room we are in. He starts speaking to me and, in his clinical, superior tone, informs me that he is going to show me pictures and that I should tell him what I see. He claims he is my friend, and I can tell him anything.*

*But that line stopped working for me early in my young life because of everything I've been through. No one can be trusted. He begins showing me Rorschach drawings, expecting some great revelation from my replies as to how disturbed of a child I really am. Much to his disappointment, I don't think seeing two hippos kissing is exactly what he is looking for. I'm terribly bored with the entire experience, and all I feel is fear and anger. Next, he brings out a series of very dramatic black-and-white Victorian-themed pictures, which are so obviously shown to get me to 'talk.' "Tell me the story of the pictures," he says.*

*As my anger grows, so does my stubbornness, and I'm*

*determined to be uncooperative. I'm not the perpetrator. Why am I being subjected to this? He is showing me a picture of a young girl lying on a sofa. Standing behind the sofa is a man in a typical melodramatic pose with the back of his hand over his eyes, turning away in shame.*

*There is no way I am saying what I see because I know what he expects me to say. I tell him I am not saying it, and I don't! He knows! That man just molested his daughter! I am not going to say it!*

*I can see the disappointment on my mother's face when I am brought back into the lobby, but I do not care. I refuse to see the psychologist ever again.*

I am the eldest of six children. My mom and dad met while working at the local newspaper, where my dad was a linotype operator, '60s cool and handsome who rode with the Hell's Angels, and my mom loved him to a fault. She eventually left the paper to work in retail.

My dad worked nights, and my Mom worked days, which meant I had to take care of my siblings during the daytime so my father could sleep. I was a good kid who essentially performed the duties of a wife and mother from the age of six years old.

I genuinely loved my parents, which would cause me a great deal of mental anguish when I got older as I tried to process what

they'd put me through. They worked hard, and we always had a nice place to live. For some reason, we moved around a lot; thirty-two times, in fact, between my birth and leaving home. This made stability in school and making friends difficult.

When I was six years old, we lived in Haslett, Michigan. It was a nice place. I went to St. Thomas Aquinas School. I loved going to school and was always a good student. I got my first dog there – a little Scottish Terrier I named Angus Fungus. I adored him, and he followed me everywhere.

We had a huge field behind our house with lots of playground equipment, including a train, a merry-go-round, a swing set, and a swimming pool. The best part was the "paths to nowhere" that were mowed in the grass so we could escape and hide in the tall grass when we did not want to be bothered. I had a group of friends in the neighborhood, and we used to put on shows in their garage. I had a lovely playhouse until we got another dog named Freckles. My dad decided my playhouse was perfect for the dog, and it became a doghouse. One day, the field caught on fire, and it burned down the playhouse. I was glad.

My dad was a hunter, which I detested. He tried to interest me in it and forced me to use a rifle one day. I shot the rifle, and a little bird fell out of a tree. That was the last time I would use a gun. I cried and cried and cried over this little sparrow, and honestly, I never forgave him. He used to come home from his hunting trips

with deer strapped to the hood of the car or a bunch of bunnies tied together at the feet—pure carnage. I never had an appetite for the meat, and it used to piss him off, so my mother would lie to me about what we were eating. I am positive my father took great delight in seeing the horror on my face after I ate a piece of "chicken" he then revealed was actually a rabbit. This sick, sadistic little game of his carried on for much of my childhood.

My parents were of the school that "You cannot leave the table until you clean your plate! There are children starving in Africa!" Well, they could have mine because I sure as hell wasn't going to eat it. I was quite stubborn, even back then, and would often sit at the table for hours until bedtime without eating a single morsel. I didn't really mind sitting alone because it gave me time to think. It was during one of these thinking sessions that I realized I could just cut my food into pill-size bites and swallow without tasting it. I was so pleased with myself that I'd found a solution. Battle won! I was a warrior child.

We moved to Bakersfield, California, when I was seven years old, but the food fights and my father's sadism continued. My parents liked having parties. Dad was a raging alcoholic who liked to be a 'big shot,' and Mom was just along for the ride. When this happened, all the kids that came with their parents got locked in a bedroom with myself and my siblings while the adults drank and partied.

Usually, the bill of fare at these parties involved seafood, which, to this day, I detest. It was at one of these parties that I became the entertainment. My dad came to the room I was in and told me to come out to the party. He had the bright idea that his friends would like to see me suffer as much as he did, and he forced me to eat food I did not like. Oysters were the worst. I was also given Scotch and beer to wash it down with. The partygoers would laugh, and then I was sent back to the room with the other kids. After that, I became a regular feature at his parties. I wish I had known the term "sick fuck" back then because it fit him perfectly.

Bakersfield was a turning point in my life. When I was about eight years old, my mother got a job in a drug store behind the cosmetics counter. It was great! She'd bring home the old perfume displays, and we used them to play with our dolls. Due to a bad run of babysitters, eventually, the responsibility of looking after the family came to me. For as long as I could remember, I changed diapers and helped with the kids. I was raised to be a back-up mother. This might have been okay if I hadn't had the added job of being a wife, too. I cooked, cleaned, and took care of my dad and brothers and sisters.

My father was tyrannical when it came to order and discipline. He ruled with a military-style that was creatively sadistic when it came to disciplining his children. How could I have known that in about thirty years, I would get some of my best cruelties for my sessions from him? I lived in a constant state of fear. When we were

called, we had to answer immediately wherever we were, no matter what we were doing. "Coming, Daddy!"

His favorite was the "Get on your knees and hold out your arms" gem. If your arms went down, you were spanked. I got to the point where I would rather have the spanking than go through all that nonsense.

He was a big believer in the belt. He relished seeing the fear on our little faces as he ceremoniously unbuckled his belt while telling us what horrible children we were. He didn't just take off the belt; he did the quick pull, which snapped when it came out of the loops. And the piece de resistance was the "fold over and snap" right before the strike. There was no finesse involved; he was just happy wherever it landed.

He was very physically cruel to my little brother Joe; God rest his soul. He used everything imaginable on him, including electric cords, which was a horror to watch. Joe was only three years old when my father had boxing matches with him and turned it into a family affair. We all had to watch this. It brings tears to my eyes whenever I think of it. Joe was a beautiful boy who would grow up not having a chance in life because of all the abuse my father inflicted upon him. Joe grew up with a lot of problems and spent most of his time in jail, which is where he seemed the happiest. Joe was a gifted carpenter and artist. We would see him on occasion, but he always seemed to want to be alone. Someone apparently found

him under a bridge in Sacramento dying. None of the family even knew until four months after his death. It was heartbreaking because you could not help him or fix things for him, which I guess is the case for most of my family. Most of us are not close, which is very sad to me.

Even though my father was especially cruel to Joe, the rest of us experienced his wrath as well. My father liked scaring me. He had a motorcycle and insisted upon taking me for rides, which I was totally opposed to, but "good girls must do what they are told." He used to take the corners and make the bike lean as much as possible around the corner, which terrified me. This did not stop him, of course; it only made it more fun for him. I was terrified of planes, too, which was another fear he liked to exploit. He had a friend who had a Cessna airplane that he used to take me up in. They liked to make me cry by taking the plane up and dropping it quickly. "Pulling Gs," they called it. I thought I was going to die, but they just thought it was funny. I would cry in sheer terror, but that did not move them; it inspired them. How sick is that?

Like many of my childhood memories, I feel like there is more to this than my mind will let me see. Why was I in an airplane with two grown men alone who wanted to terrorize and torture me?

Luckily, sometimes, our minds block certain things out to protect us. I'm thankful for that.

But there are so many painful memories of my father that my

mind hasn't blocked out. One involves nail-biting. I was a habitual nail-biter growing up. My father's cure for this compulsion of mine was to get out a metal nail file and a small bowl of alcohol. He would file my nails down until they bled and then dip them in the alcohol. I know the alcohol was not to prevent infection – it was to hurt me. This was a beginning insight into my future stubbornness, as I refused to stop biting my nails, no matter how much he tortured me. Eventually, he became bored with the whole thing, and I grew up to be a happy nail-biter who stopped when she was damned good and ready.

One day, after making my father's lunch while Mom was at work, I was called into Dad's room to "scratch his back." I was eight years old. My father always ran around in his Jockey shorts, which bothered me as long as I can remember, and today was no different. That day, he decided it was his fatherly duty to introduce me to *Playboy* magazine. It was the issue with Marilyn Monroe in it. I can still feel the uneasiness I felt at that moment, trying to understand why he was showing me this. He thumbed through the magazine until he came to the centerfold, which he claimed I needed to see. I was absolutely confused and clueless as to how we went from back-scratching to this. He wanted me to lie next to him so he could "cuddle me." It felt wrong, but *he was my father so it must be right, right?* It was not a nice cuddle; it felt dirty and wrong. He took my hand and put it on his erect penis over his Jockey shorts, and I can, to this day, feel the panic and confusion. As I write this, I have

anxiety and trouble breathing. He proclaimed it was a father's duty to teach his daughters what to do to make men happy. This is my first vivid memory of my abuse, which continued until I was 12 years old. *Stop and breathe.* I did not tell my mother because *while it was what fathers were supposed to do, mothers should not know and would not understand.*

Eventually, we ended up leaving California and moving to St. Louis, where Dad's parents lived. I was in 5th grade now, which I remember clearly because that was the year President Kennedy was shot.

Dad got a job at the *St Louis Post Dispatch*, and we lived with my grandparents for a while. At first, I was excited because I was my grandmother's favorite. She was pretty obvious about it, which did not endear me to my five younger brothers and sisters.

But the joy soon seeped out of living with my grandparents. When you live with someone, you learn a lot about them, and it is not always good. I slept on a cot in their room. The first time my grandmother changed her clothes in front of me, I was mortified. Then came the added bonus of my grandfather. He was a real creep who liked to run around in his boxer shorts and, when no one was looking, slipped his hand into his fly, pulled out his disgusting appendage, and waved it at me while wiggling his tongue at me. I remember wondering if his eyes would pop out of their sockets because they got so big when he was doing it.

It was a great day when we got our own house. It was a rental since my parents were having a house custom-built in the suburbs. But I really loved it because it was on a pond and there were woods behind the house, which I spent a lot of time in. I decided I was a poet at ten, so I would go into the woods alone with a notebook and write my little poems. I loved the solitude and felt very important and grown up, being a poet and all. We used to camp out in our station wagon, go fishing early in the morning, and have fish for breakfast. It was so nice. Things seemed a little less scary while we lived there. I don't know if the set-up of the house was not conducive to night-time rendezvous with your prepubescent daughter, or maybe my dad was just working too much. I did not care why… I just felt a little safer for a little while, perhaps because I had an escape route! Once the dreamhouse was finished, we all moved in.

Shit!

The new house and the new state did not make our lives any better. The abuse continued, and there were more of us now to torture.

I was in seventh grade now, and I loved going to school. This year was the first time I was in a public school, and I made a lot of friends and was almost one of the cool kids. My boyfriend was the class president, and my father had a cow when he found out we were sitting together on the bus and holding hands in school. I got in so much trouble. I was told I was not allowed to have a boyfriend, much

less sit with him or hold hands. This is when I hated myself the most. How the hell would they know if I did hold hands with him? But because I was so scared all of the time, I had to break it off. He was really nice, and we continued our relationship without the perks. My first good guy! Terry Mitchell.

At home, I lived in a constant state of fear, unable to sleep at night but pretending to do so when he came into my room. I slept in a room with my three sisters. The room was dormitory style with bunk beds for all of us. I would usually hear fighting from my parents' bedroom across the hall and lots of "No, Larry!" These were words I dreaded most because I knew he would be coming for me soon. I tried so hard to become invisible or pretend to sleep so deeply that I could not be awakened. He entered the room and went from bed to bed, looking at my sisters, sometimes touching them while I pretended harder to be asleep. My heart was beating so fast, and I was sure he could hear it as he went from bed to bed.

The result, no matter how hard I wished it away, was being taken out of my bed and into the living room, where I had to be quiet or "I would get in trouble with Mom." I had to be quiet, which was absurd because I had just heard my mother turning my father down in her bedroom. We had Colonial furniture with those stupid wagon wheels on the ends of the couch. He was always on top of me, and I could not breathe. The grunting sounds he made still ring in my ears.

I was busty for my age, and he used to knead my breasts while

taking credit for their size like he was doing me a monumental favor of sorts. He always assured me I would thank him when I grew up because the boys liked girls with big tits. I can still recall the fear I felt these nights and days and the disgust of hearing his noises in my ears. It has never left me.

I often wondered how my mother could have been so blind to what was going on. As I got older and smarter, I started to see things that made her behavior very obvious to me, and by the time I was in the 7th grade, I knew for sure my mother knew what was going on.

I went to Catholic school most of my life except for that year when I was in public school. I had joined the Pep Club. It was my first game night, and my mother was going to take me to the game. I was dressed in my red skirt, white blouse, white knee socks, and red Keds with my hair in pigtails with red ribbons. I was so excited to be going. I came into the living room to let my parents know I was ready, and then the air was sucked out of the room.

My mother told me she could not take me and that my father would be doing so. I asked why, and she had no reason. I started to cry and told her I did not want to go; I begged her to take me, and she wouldn't. I told her I did not want to go anymore and that I would stay home. She told me to quit being so dramatic and go with my father. Once he said, "Let's go," I wanted to die. He took me to the creek before he took me to the game. This was the night I learned what a condom was. He had condoms in the glove compartment of

the car. I did not know what a condom was until that night. He opened it up, gave it to me, and made me put it on him. I was so revolted by the way it all felt. I quit Pep Club the next day.

Later that year, the shit hit the fan. Two black station wagons appeared in the middle of the night when my father was at work. We were all loaded into the cars with none of our precious belongings, no explanation, just terror in our hearts, not knowing where we were going or what was going on. Our precious big white fluffy dog was left at the top of the stairs, never to be seen again. To this day, I am still angry that I could not take my Beatles card collection!

This trip was planned by my mother and my uncle, who had been packing for weeks after a neighbor had told my mother that my father had molested one of her daughters at my sleepover. I'd been called into the kitchen and asked, "What the hell is going on?!" *Maybe ask your husband, who has been molesting me for six years. Yeah, I am the bad guy here!* Even at a young age, I felt this tone was misdirected at me. Or did she think I did something?

We drove all night and rarely stopped along the way. I could feel the sense of urgency to get out of Missouri and land wherever we were going. I remember lying in the back of the car, looking at the stars out of the back window as we drove. The car was incredibly quiet for all the passengers in it. The only sounds came from the crackly car radio, and it was country music the whole way, which I detested. Like life wasn't bad enough already!

When we arrived in Michigan, two of my sisters, one of my brothers, and I were put in a Catholic children's home. Meanwhile, my two youngest siblings stayed with my mother in my grandparents' house.

The children's home was a place that horror films are modeled after, but it was deceptive to outsiders because everything seemed copacetic during visiting hours. The nuns were mean, and the male counselor was a sadistic asshole who liked to beat on the boys and peek into the girls' showers. It was awful. The building was sterile, with tile floors and high ceilings, so the sounds of children crying at night echoed throughout the hallways. It made one feel so desperate and alone.

There was always food! So much food! We, of course, were not allowed to leave the table until we finished our plate. That, along with the mounds of chocolate that were given to us daily, gave me a nice weight gain of 40 pounds in nine months. I have struggled with my weight every day since then.

My grandfather despised me and blamed me for "seducing" my father and essentially breaking up my parents' marriage. I was not allowed in his house, which complicated things a bit with the rest of the family. On the few occasions he had to let me in, we simply did not speak. He smoked these awful cigars that made me feel sick, and he always had one in his mouth… that soggy, nasty stub just hanging out of his mouth.

After about a year, my grandfather bought my mother a small house in Lansing, which I know she probably hated, but she had no other options. He would own her for the rest of his life now.

I don't remember ever seeing my mother smile after the divorce. She never stopped loving my father, which was very confusing to me, but I guess it should not have been, considering that in her eyes, I was responsible for what happened. Who knew one could be such a seductress at the age of 6? How sick. I used to come downstairs in the middle of the night and find her alone in the living room in the dark. You could only see the glow of the end of her cigarette as she smoked, and Jim Croce's tunes reinforced her misery.

My mother also managed to land a job as the school secretary at my high school, which really put a damper on my social life. It was the '60s man! I was supposed to be protesting, doing sit-ins, and going to San Francisco to get some flowers in my hair. Instead, I had no real life to speak of. I started working at the age of 12, cleaning houses and ironing sheets for rich people during summer vacation to earn money to pay for my school books and uniforms, which was the last thing I wanted to spend my hard-earned money on. I could not participate in after-school activities because I was the eldest child and had to go home and take care of my siblings, which was really a joke as no one ever listened to me. *Why would they?*

I had a small group of friends in high school, the "Not the Cool

Kids" group. Eventually, I figured out that most of us came from broken homes and were just instinctively drawn to each other. My best friend was Janice, and as I got a little older, I was able to hang out with her and have sleepovers. We listened to records and played a game called "Under the Blanket" with our 45s. The way the game worked was to say the name of the record and add the words "under the blanket." The purpose of the game was to make it sexual… like "Touch Me In the Morning – Under the Blanket." We were boy-crazy teenagers who had not even had our first kiss yet. It seemed so salacious to us at the time.

The best thing was sneaking copies of Cosmopolitan into her house and soaking in all the information we could glean from the pages of this scandalous magazine while we ate potato chips with French onion dip. These were my good times. We were gloriously stupid together, hanging out at the playground waiting for the hot janitor to come to work, walking to the mini-market for a cold bottle of Pepsi, and dressing ourselves as matching pimples for Halloween one year. It was so great to feel those fleeting moments of freedom.

As I said, I was very boy-crazy. I loved the Monkees and James Taylor, as I still do to this day! I did not really date guys from my school except one: Bob V. Bob was tall, kind, and handsome. I was very uncomfortable with my sexuality and very awkward. I got up the nerve to ask him to the Sadie Hawkins dance one year, and he accepted. Best day ever! The dance was great, and then he kissed

21

me. I had never been kissed by a boy. My reaction was not good…
in fact, it was humiliating. My gut told me to run, and I did. I ran
away straight to the ladies' room crying, and I vomited. Worst day
ever! I never dated any of the boys from school again.

When I turned 16, I got my first real job at Hot Sam's Pretzels
in a kiosk in the middle of the mall. It was a great spot located across
from the 8-track tape kiosk, the cool shoe store, and Chess King,
which was a men's hippie-type clothing store. I used to lust after the
suede stars-and-stripes vest with the long fringe on it. It was
fabulous!

I was in a different world where no one really knew me, and I
could finally be me. I discovered people liked me and that I was
smart, clever, and kind of cute, too. I met a lot of cool people and
was a little star in the mall. The guys at the shoe store called me
Bubbles La Rue from the Boom Boom Room.

I never knew if that was a good thing or not, but I did like the
name Bubbles, and I loved the attention. The best day ever was when
the older, handsome, bearded hippie dude running the 8-track tape
kiosk asked me out. I did not know or care where we were going; I
just thought I was the shit because he asked me. We ended up at a
little house on a lake. I was not even there for 15 minutes yet, and
he already had me in the bedroom on my back, dry-humping me. I
just lay there, not knowing what the fuck was going on. I was almost
laughing inside because I just did not get it. He went from coolest

guy ever to creep, and the best day ever turned out not so great in a heartbeat!

Eventually, my days at the pretzel stand ended when the manager of a toy store across from the pretzel stand, who liked my work ethic, invited me to work for him. I was all over it, so I took the job and loved it.

In my last year of high school, I was working one day when two interesting characters came into the store to buy a squirt gun. They were precisely the kind of guys you could not take home to the parents! They were both wearing purple corduroy pants with pink pockets and were having a laugh while they shopped. One was a skinny guy with brown greaser hair, and the other a 6'1" blonde-haired, blue-eyed guy with a twinkle in his eye that spelled trouble. He was handsome and charming, and he had me at "Hello, sweet thang, you have to come over to my ride!"

*A carnie! How perfect!*

# FIRST LOVE

I went to the carnival outside the mall and hopped on the Himalayas. It was all so exciting. This dreamy boy named George liked me. Draggin' the Line by Tommy James of the Shondells was playing as the ride began to move and pick up speed. Suddenly, he appeared out of nowhere, jumped on my car, and rode around on the outside of it, chatting me up and making me laugh. It was totally a knight-in-shining-armor situation for me! He was hilarious and made me feel good. We clicked right away. I spent every second I could with him while he was there.

My friend had a car, and we used to stop at the store to get a bottle of Boones Farm and some snacks. I was still a total goody-goody, so my bill of fare was grape juice and Ding Dongs! There was not a lot going on in Lansing, Michigan, so we spent a lot of time in country cemeteries, scaring ourselves and having a good time.

The night before he had to go, I was so sad, and I had my first official sexual experience in the back of an 18-wheeler. It was quick; I did not get all the fuss about it, but he was happy. He left the next day, and I got my letter-writing fingers in shape to make up for his absence. I wrote to him every day because that is what teenage girls do. He did not reciprocate but he did call me from the road.

Once the season was over, he came and got me. I did not know where I was going, nor did I care. I was getting the hell out of town and going on a great adventure. He took me to Detroit for the weekend. I was just happy to be with him. It was so romantic sitting in the car next to him with his big, muscly arm around me, listening to tunes on the radio of the Ford Fairlane he was driving. The car was black with a red interior and went by the name Midnight Rambler. We got to Detroit, and I stuck to him like glue. All of his friends were there, and we all just hung out and had a good time. I saw parts of Detroit I did not know existed on this trip, with tenement buildings and lots of poverty where we stayed. Three days later, he dropped me off on the corner by my house. Not cool, *but who cared at that age?*

When I got home, I found myself locked out of my house and slept on the back porch. Things were not good at home, but I cherished every phone call I got from him. He came up to visit from time to time, but he never stayed or met my mother. About two months after the drop-off, I found myself going to the deli in the mall for hot fudge sundaes and giant garlic pickles. People started teasing me about being pregnant. This was not something that ever crossed my mind, but I realized that I probably needed to be checked out. It was difficult because there were no home-pregnancy kits back then, and I could not go to the family doctor, so I just decided I was.

At about four months, I told my mother I was pregnant, and she

kicked me out of the house, which was fine. I had an independent streak in me and a job, so I got a small apartment and went on with my life. I am sure I did not fully understand how much my life was about to change.

I did not tell George I was pregnant. The last thing I wanted in life was to be someone who had to get married because she was pregnant. I loved him so much, but I was not going to be in a situation where he felt forced to marry me. I knew if he didn't, I would be able to take care of the baby alone. The good thing was that he did ask me to marry him, and I accepted. When I told him about the baby, he was happy and decided to join the military to get us on our feet. He and his pal went in on the buddy system, so they were based together.

We were so young. I was so happy when I was pregnant with my daughter. I was never happier in my life than at that time. We lived on base, and I was spoiled by the airmen who were always looking out for me. His Air Force career was short. He did not like it and did everything he could to get out of his service. He stopped having his uniforms cleaned or pressed and did not dress appropriately. This looked bad since I washed them in the bathtub. Base housing was pretty subpar, and the pay was not great, so we could not afford much. They weren't buying it and made him stay, and surprisingly, they put up with his disregard for duty.

He and his friend spent a great deal of time out at night, and he

came home one night without his shoes. He had left them at the brothel he and his buddy had been to. My mother had not been well, and he hatched a plan to get a hardship discharge, saying we were needed to help my mother. This was a big fat lie since I had five brothers and sisters, all younger than me, to care for her. But his plan worked, and we ended up back in Michigan.

We had three children by the time I was 22. IIe was a truck driver and struggled to keep a job because he was young and always on the bottom of the totem pole. I always worked because his income, while good, was unreliable. As time went on, the marriage started to fail. There was lots of anger and frustration on both sides, and my BDSM inclinations, which I had been stifling for years, were becoming a real need for me.

When the Story of O came out, I asked him to take me to the movie. He had no idea what it was about, but if it was porn, he was down for it. He was angry after the movie and told me how sick and disgusting it was. I had just found my hero and, from that day forward, wanted to be O. Seeing the movie strengthened my desire for submission, and one night, I took a belt to bed and begged him to use it on me. This went over like a lead balloon! He just lost it, and that was the beginning of the end for us.

We left Michigan shortly after his discharge from the Air Force and moved to Pearl River, Louisiana, or as I liked to call it, my own personal hell! We moved in with George's parents, who were both

raging alcoholics. I hated it there and welcomed the day I could get a job working for Miss Dot at the local Quick Stop and get some peace away from home. Adapting to the differences in my way of life was not easy for me, and I fought every step of the way. The town was in the backwoods near the Mississippi border, and it consisted of a post office, jail, a local general store, and a Piggly Wiggly.

I saw with my own eyes that the South had not changed much from its Antebellum ways, and those in power wielded it with gusto. It made me sad to see and feel the acceptance of this way of life and the implied subservience of diverse backgrounds to "The Man." I had to stifle my Yankee beliefs and suck it up. I was the only one in the house working at times, and the day I came home to find a hog head in a pot cooking on the stove, I lost my shit. I had to get out of there. Everyone is entitled to live life the way they want, but this was not my choice.

Not soon enough, we moved into a horrible single-wide mobile home for $90 a month. It was like living in an oven in the hot, humid weather. George landed a good job working for a reputable truck company as a driver, which he later gave up to start a pizza delivery service in Slidell, Louisiana. We had a brisk business, but it was not enough, and soon, we were not able to make payment on the loan he got from a man named Mr. Gambino.

We had to pack up late one night and then headed to California.

I was not sad about this. This was my dream situation because my sister lived there, and I had planned to divorce my husband in California. California Dreamin'!

We officially split up the day I came home from work, and the babysitter was sitting on his lap. To add insult to injury, she was the sister-in-law of my little sister. That was it for me. A monster inside of me was released when I saw this walking down the path to the front door, and I just lost it. I was going to "kill the bitch," as they say. My husband came out to try and calm me down, which was never going to happen. I started to try to kick his ass. Mind you, he is 6'1" and 200 pounds, and I was not.

It was surely a comical scene to behold while I windmilled my arms, trying to reach him, and he held me away with one arm. The police were called, and they had to escort the bitch out of the house. This was a shock to me, and it had been going on for some time. Later, I laughed, remembering how he always used to tell me that when God passed out looks, he hit her in the face with a frying pan. I was done!

# THE JOURNEY

After we split, we shared custody of our children. We were both in the same city, and I had the kids with me, and he visited them when he was not working. I was working a full-time job as well. He paid the rent on the apartment we stayed in. My life changed forever when he told me he was moving to Oregon with the babysitter and taking the kids! I did not believe it at first. How could he do that? No matter what my situation in life has been, being a mother was what brought me the most joy.

My kids kept me on the straight and narrow and inspired me every day to keep going. One of the most brutal days of my life was putting my three children on an airplane to go and stay with their dad. I felt my heart would explode. Before the flight, they went to the gift shop and came back with a little stuffed white ball of fur with a nose, feet, and arms. They gave me "Bosco" to take care of me while they were away. From that day on, any time one of us was separated, Bosco went with us.

When my kids were not with me, I lost my way. The desolation I felt was soul-destroying. My children were my life, my purpose, and my joy. I worked and went home to an empty house. I became very depressed and did not really care about myself or my well-being. I did not have much self-esteem to begin with, being raised in the school of "children should be seen and not heard." I had no

one I could trust, which was an ongoing theme in my life even to this day. I suppose not being able to trust the people who brought you into this world is not a good start to developing trust.

Eventually, I began to go out a little bit. I had a work friend who introduced me to a couple of her friends, and I fell in love with them immediately. James and Adam introduced me to some of the best gay dance clubs in town. They shared with me the joys of Santa Monica Boulevard and a whole new world to explore. I found Circus of Books, which became my go-to source of information. We became very close quickly, and it was by hanging out with them that I learned to feel I was an okay person. I loved the freedom they seemed to enjoy by not giving a flying fuck what anyone thought and how they just knew how to have fun.

I had never experienced the freedom of being myself. I began to wear a collar and dress in fetish clothes and handcuffs. They loved it, and I reveled in the attention I got when I presented my true self to the world. James and I had the same taste in men, which was a hoot. I was super shy, so he would scout for me and bring me the boy! It was great! We dressed in themes when we went out and never missed Dynasty Thursday at Circus.

It was exhilarating to dance all night and into the morning. We would start at Circus, move to The Rage, and then do after-hours at Catch One or go to church on Sunday morning at Greg's Blue Dot, where the boys danced with abandon with fans. It was a beautiful

thing. These guys were so important to me in shaping who I would later become.

Eventually, I became confident enough to go out on my own, and I danced five nights a week. I knew most of the bouncers and felt safe. All of this was a wonderful distraction from the pain I was feeling inside. I felt like the worst mother in the world. I began not to care what happened to me, and I started living dangerously and doing stupid things.

The longer I was away from my kids, the worse my mindset became, and I started to sow all the wild oats I missed sowing when I was younger. I began going to strip clubs. The people who ran the clubs I attended were always happy to see me. I liked to dress up when I went out. One of the ladies told me I classed up the joint. I rarely had to buy a drink.

The nights I could not go out with my friends, I just went alone. I became pretty promiscuous at this point. I felt numb inside and did not really care too much about what happened to me. Don't get me wrong, I had some amazing adventures when I became super daring. I became the darling of the male strippers and was never wanting for a one-night stand.

I was very naïve and trusting, which is attractive to men of a certain ilk. Some might call it stupid, which, in retrospect, I agree with. I don't know how I managed to live through this and never got hurt. I was able to take the emotional aspect out of sex and had more

of a male attitude towards it. Love had not worked out so well for me, so why not?

I met a man named Grant, who was my first BDSM experience. He was a tall, attractive man with a beard and beautiful eyes. We dated a few times, and I felt I could trust him. Keeping in mind that I had decided I was O incarnate, I was up for anything because that is what a good submissive does.

One night, I let him tie me up in a chair. I was excited and scared. Finally! Someone got me. It turned out his toy of choice was a rubber hose! Not a great starting point for a newbie, but I took it, and I took it quietly, as a good submissive would. A rubber hose hurts like hell and tends to leave marks when wielded by a giant of a man. When he was done, we talked for a while, and he left. He never called again.

I decided to buy a flogger and hang it up in my living room. It was a real ice-breaker. Some people who came into the house would look at it and pretend it wasn't there, and those who dared to say something were usually intrigued but not sure what they should think about it.

One night, it finally got used. I was coming home from a night out with my guys, and I saw at a bus stop two adorable boys who looked like they had just left prom and were taking the bus home. They were wearing the very popular baby blue tuxedo with the ruffled shirt of the time. So, it was either a prom or a wedding.

I was stopped at the light, and they saw me and started boyish shenanigans, trying to get my attention, which they did. They asked for a ride, and I said sure. They were too cute. We ended up back at my place, and I spent the weekend with them. I was insatiable in those days, so between the two of them, I got my flogging, enough sex to last me for weeks, and breakfast to boot on Sunday morning. After breakfast, I took them to the bus stop and never saw them again. These were my Hollywood boys, and they were amazing.

# LEARNING THE ROPES

Once I had my first introduction to BDSM and knew it was a real thing and not just in my mind, I became obsessed with learning everything I could about it. I bought every book I could find on the subject and began to educate myself and read some really great stories as well.

I had already fallen in love with The Story of O by Pauline Réage. There were so many more great books I discovered that were both informative and sexy to read. I think one of the most common series newbies read at the time was the Sleeping Beauty series by A.N. Roquelaure, who we learned later was Anne Rice. This was a series of three books beautifully written and full of great fantasies.

I discovered a series of science-fiction books written by John Norman that were not the best reads but were titillating fantasy for a new submissive. Gor was a planet where women were slaves, of course. I read a few of them and still have them today. Gor was a pretty heavy scene. I tried going on a Gor chat room once, and I failed miserably even to get in because you had to know all the terminology and how to slither in on your belly and beg for entrance. The stories were tripe, but I liked them. When I discovered there

were 19 Gor positions, I learned every one of them and added that to my list of being an interesting and educated submissive.

Another good read was *'Exit to Eden'* by Anne Rampling, who was also later revealed to be Anne Rice. If you have seen the movie and not read the book, you should forget about the movie and read some good BDSM fiction instead. The movie sucked… it was a joke!

9 ½ Weeks by Elizabeth McNeil was a super sexy read for me, and who could have asked for more when a movie came out with Mickey Rourke and Kim Bassinger in it? It was a sexy movie, but for some reason, the guys always have to be sickos in the end, and the poor women are victims. This is a common theme in a lot of BDSM fiction. I could easily relate to the characters in the movies, yet at the same time, I was frustrated by their reactions. The women are hapless morons who need to be saved by a man or are so stupid they cannot figure out whether they want to be tied up or not, so they submit and hate themselves for it later, and the guy is a jerk. Give me a break and give women some credit!

In the January 13, 2015 issue of The Atlantic, Merissa Gerson wrote: "BDSM was considered aberrant behavior. It was not until 2010 that The American Psychiatric Association announced it

would be changing the diagnostic codes for BDSM, fetishism, and transvestic fetishism in the next edition of its Diagnostic and Statistical Manual of Mental Disorders, published in 2013. Consenting adults were no longer deemed mentally ill for choosing sexual behavior outside the mainstream."

Ah, what would we all do without the mainstream to guide us to righteous behavior?

# WHERE'S YOUR MASTER?

BDSM has been a massive part of who I am even before I could define it. Puberty was when it began to emerge. When I was a teenager, all my fantasies involved me in a powerless position, submitting to a higher authority. I guess you don't have to be a rocket scientist to put my childhood and my proclivity toward submission together to figure out what led me to kink.

Of course, I thought there was something wrong with me. I still wonder to this day why I did not put myself in a position of power. It was only later in life that I discovered *I was in the power position, as a submissive.*

Yes, it is an age-old story… A girl sexually, physically, and mentally abused by her parents turns to BDSM and grows up with masochistic tendencies. While I fit the stereotype, please be sure many people into kink come from very loving families and lead very "normal" lives.

I just happened to hit the dysfunction jackpot! I always was an overachiever. Therapy was what the doctor ordered at the time for my "aberrant proclivities," and saving me from myself was the goal of every therapist I ever saw. I had a terrible track record with therapists. I never liked them, and our relationships were always short-lived. The last woman I saw sat in front of me, asking me all the usual stupid questions I had heard before, but this time, I had a

major revelation inside myself.

She asked me, "Why do you like being a slave? Why do you like being hurt?" The answer came to me like manna from heaven… "Why don't you?" This was an awakening for me that everyone's normal is not the same and that this had been a normal part of my life for as long as I could remember, so why was I trying to fight it? Because other people thought I was sick? Because I was going to go to hell? Who were they to judge? I let her know we were done and I would not be returning but thanked her for her help. I remember feeling a weight lifted off my shoulders at that moment; I felt relief and no shame for who I was.

I was still going out with my boys. I loved the adoration they showed me and their acceptance and friendship. There were no clubs or places for kinksters in the late '70s, but we were welcomed into the gay community.

I began going to swingers clubs with some of the men I "dated." The ridiculous thing about this was I was not a swinger nor bisexual. I was just kinky, but being a good little submissive, whatever he wanted, I would accommodate. Back in those days, men could not get into a swingers club without a lady, so I was their ticket to the event. The funny thing was that I usually had more fun than they did. They usually ended up pissed off by the end of the evening because I was more in demand, and they were walking around like a tool looking for something to do. The best thing that ever happened

was the time a group of men and women locked me in a room with them and locked my date out. What could I do? I was tied to a bedspread eagle and unable to open the door! It was glorious!

Occasionally, I would find someone kinky and was able to play. There was a swingers bar in La Mirada called the Den that I started frequenting, and I would go by myself because I knew people now and felt safe. One night, I was walking to the ladies' room. I was wearing my collar as always, and as I passed by the bar, I noticed a beautiful blonde woman sitting on top of the bar. I remember her moccasin boots since I love fringe! I kept walking, and then I heard those words… the words that opened the door to my fantasy world, the words that sent a chill up my spine, the words that made my heart sing and struck just a tiny bit of terror in it simultaneously: "Where is your Master?"

His name was Carl, and hers was Tiffany. Tiffany was Carl's slave. I had never met a Master/slave couple, and I was thrilled. I immediately went into submissive mode. The funny thing about being naturally submissive is that you just know what to do. You don't need training; you understand and practice protocol because it is inside you, and serving brings you so much joy.

We spoke for a while, and it turned out Carl was working at a BDSM club called the Chateau, which was one of the first clubs in Los Angeles. I recalled I had seen an article about it in Time magazine when I was younger and was fascinated by it. He invited

me to come to the Chateau to work. I was not sure I was ready for that, but there were other offerings. Sir James, who owned the Chateau, ran meetings one Sunday a month for the "Order of Roissy," and I went to one of those to check things out. I felt right at home, but my boyfriend at the time was intimidated by the whole thing, so we did not return. The room we met in was a simple meeting room. There was no equipment in it. These meetings seemed to be purely informational. The most exciting thing about the meeting was when his slave, Kiana, would enter the room. She was a beautiful blonde dressed to the nines in Trashy Lingerie. I loved/hated her the first time I saw her. I did not attend many of these meetings. I found them a little tedious once the initial thrill was gone.

Being submissive with no guidance can lead to all kinds of stupid moves. I suspect this is because part of your nature is to please people, and saying "no" does not come easily. Combine that with a history of abuse, and the abuse just seemed to continue. I am always amazed at the ignorance of people who shame women for staying in bad situations. "Why didn't you just leave?" The answer is simple. It is all you know. I was a magnet for abusive men. At the time, I did not realize I was being abused… I just felt that this is the way it is for women, and to suck it up and do what you are supposed to do. Stand by your man and all that!

This boyfriend was just one of an extensive line of abusive men

I ended up with. He was not physically abusive, but he was mentally and financially abusive. Eventually, I figured out he had another girlfriend and child but came to me every Thursday to get money, which I later found out he was using for prostitutes.

I wanted to go to the Chateau for a session, and when my birthday came around that year, he told me he would take me. I got all dressed up and was ready to go, but he called to cancel on me. I let him have it on the phone and made him feel guilty, so he finally agreed to take me. I told him to go fuck himself and that I was not going. I knew he was coming over, so I changed into my pajamas and my bunny slippers. When he arrived, he forced me to get dressed, which I did, but I refused to put my shoes on, so he dragged me out to the car in my beautiful dress and bunny slippers. He made me keep my head down in the car and we drove to West Hollywood to the Chateau. He took me in. It was a weird time then. While BDSM is consensual and all that, it seems that the only one who needed to consent to this interaction was the guy who brought me.

I was taken to a dungeon and told to strip. He stayed in the room to watch. Enter one beautiful African American Domina. Her name was Mistress Deidre. We were a match: I was stubborn as hell, and she was determined to break me. I was given a safe word before the session began, and that was about it. No questions about what I liked or didn't like or what my limits were. I would not have given them anyway. The session was a battle. She put alligator clips on my nipples. I had never had any kind of clamp on my nipples. They were

left on the entire one-hour session. Let's just say she used every piece of equipment at her disposal and loved beating the crap out of me and trying to get me to say "mercy." I don't know why I was so stubborn, but I was. This was my first session ever, and I was going to win! No mercy for me! This was a trait that would stay with me my entire submissive career. My breasts were black and blue, and so were my ass and my thighs. She ended up shoving her boot heel up my ass as a send-off and told me to keep the nipple clamps on until I got home and showered. The drive home was about an hour. I decided about halfway home to remove the nipple clamps. I had never had nipple clamps on in my life, and I had no instruction on the best way to remove them. I took two fingers and applied pressure to open the clamps quickly and screamed at the top of my lungs in pain. I had never felt such intense pain before, and it scared the crap out of my boyfriend. I was grateful he kept the car on the road. This was my first lesson in BDSM on what *not* to do.

Weeks passed by, and I thought about my session a lot. I felt great satisfaction with myself that I was able to take so much and never give in. I wanted to be a part of the kink world, and I belonged there.

My kids had moved back to be with me for a while in California but were now living back again with their father as I was recovering from yet another abusive situation—a serious one at that. My children had been living with me and a man I had been dating for

some time. Things started out well, as they usually do in these situations. We lived in a lovely house, we both worked, and the kids were doing well in school. I cannot remember what set him off, but one night, while my kids were home, he went off on me in the bedroom. He locked the door so the kids could not get in, and he started beating me. I was down on the floor crying, and as he was kicking me, all I could think of was the terror my kids were feeling on the other side of the door. They were yelling, crying, and trying to come in to help me. It was the worst feeling in the world, feeling the pain and helplessness of my kids through that door. I don't remember what made him stop, just like I don't remember why he started in the first place. I just knew at that moment that I had to get my kids out of that house to safety. I don't even remember what I did afterward. Within a couple of days, the kids were on a plane back to their father, and I remained where I was.

I don't know why I stayed, but I did. Yet I had full intentions of figuring out a way to get out of there as quickly as I could. It is strange when you are in a situation like this. What is it that keeps us from leaving? What the hell is wrong with someone who stays with someone like this? It is a mystery to me to this day. I know I had no self-esteem and no confidence, and I felt less than. Did I think I deserved it, or was I just used to and expected nothing less from a man?

Two weeks later, I was lying in bed, missing my children and crying for them. He told me to shut up and stop crying. I could not

do that. He became incensed. He got up from the bed, went to the closet, and pulled out a shotgun. I did not know he had a gun in the house. The blessing of the night was the zipper jammed on the gun case. I had time to escape, and I ran out of the house looking for safety. I was running down the road crying in my pink lace nightgown at about 1:00 AM when a car with three young men in it stopped to see if I wanted a ride somewhere. Alarm bells should have been going off, but they weren't, as I just wanted to be safe. I asked them to take me to the police station. They took me to a motel. I could have appeared as some crazy nut running down the road, I suppose, and they thought I would be up for some fun, but when we got to the motel, they were very respectful and sympathetic to me and decided to take me to the police station.

I have always felt I had some type of higher being looking after me because I have been in some dire predicaments in my life and ended up being okay in the end. As my last therapist told me, "It's a miracle you're still alive."

I thanked them when they dropped me off, and I went inside to get help. The police wrapped me in a blanket, and I told them what happened. Here is where the stupidity continues. They wanted me to press charges, but I did not want to. **Why**? After that, there was nothing they could do for me. I called a friend to get me, and I went home and stayed with her. The next day, she went with me to help me get my things, and I left for good. The next problem was that this

man and I worked together, and he was in a position of authority. I won't go into all of it, but it did not end well for yours truly.

Or did it?

I left my job and looked for other work. I ended up in a semi-management position for a then-well-known denim store. I lived in a small, adorable apartment in Whittier, California, and got myself some furniture. I made it a feminine environment, including the floggers on the wall in the living room!

The job did not pay much, and I wanted to get myself back in a position that would allow me to have my children back with me. I continued to hang out with my friends, and I partied five nights a week. There was a local nightclub I liked going to that had male strippers every Thursday night, and I was there! I loved watching the strippers. I was highly entertained watching them gyrate and do their best to get those dollar bills. I must be honest; I did enjoy a few of them on deeper levels. When a man can suck the cream out of Twinkie while he is grinding on the floor, what's a girl to do?

One of my best nights was when a cute young man invited me over to the Pussycat Theater. He was the projectionist. He was adorable and, as it turned out, a natural Dom. Playing in the projection booth while the movies were rolling lent an element of excitement, and the danger of being caught was a great aphrodisiac! I remember my head looking out of one of the projection windows while I was on my hands and knees being flogged, and I could not

make a sound. *Amazing experience!*

The new job was a pretty "go nowhere" situation for me, so I decided to try to contact the manager of the Chateau I had met earlier to see about work. He was no longer there but told me about a club called Club O, which might work out for me. This was the first time I met Mistress Stephanie Locke, who was running the Club. She had a very grand demeanor, and I admired her confidence. She was much younger than I was, and I was impressed she had her own club. On my first night, I felt lost and had no clue what to expect or what to do. The training back in those days was to be thrown into the lion's den and see if you could make it out. I remember when I was talking to Mistress Stephanie, being interrupted by the jangle of the O rings on a set of cuffs. The sound was reminiscent of jingle bells to me. Entering the room was an adorable and very petite blonde who had left her session to ask Mistress Stephanie a question. She was coked out of her mind. I had never seen anyone on cocaine, but I knew this was it. She was twitchy and seemed stressed but happy at the same time. I was no expert, but I did later learn that cocaine was indeed her drug of choice.

My first session was with a man who had never played before, so we both looked at each other with that blank look of "WTF do we do now?" He had a leather fetish, and for some reason, on my first day as a submissive, I happened to be wearing a black leather skirt and jacket. Rookie! He was a nice man, but this was not the session

47

of my dreams for sure. He was as submissive as I was, and we ended up just rolling around on the floor so he could smell my leather. The rest of the night is a blur now. I only worked there for a couple of weeks before I had to leave because the man in my life did not like me working there. This was something I would later learn that was very commonplace in those days for the ladies who worked.

# CLUB O

Not long after I got rid of him, I went back looking to work only to learn that Master Jon and Mistress Patty had bought Club O. The

good news was that Carl and Tiffany were there. The club had also moved to a beautiful Victorian home in Hollywood on Taft and Franklin. It was stunning, and the rooms were well-appointed. It was two stories with an attic room that became the Paddles Room.

The year was 1981, and I was thrilled to find my new home. This was real old-school BDSM. To work, you had to pass a test, which was basically a session with one of the Masters of the house, and if you came out able to still walk, you passed. This was real. My fantasy was becoming a reality. The session was intense, with no holds barred, and I was proud of every bruise I had come out of that room with. It turns out I was a masochist, which I did not know existed, but I always had a high tolerance for pain. Combine that with my stubbornness and pride, and I made for a very marketable submissive.

I was hired! I was told the rules, which basically were just to do what the Doms say! The submissives in those days catered to the Dominas and Masters without question. We kept the club clean and cleaned up after the Doms. We took turns with ashtray duty. If there were more than five cigarette butts in an ashtray, that was cause for punishment. It was a glorious time. I never viewed being submissive as a path to becoming Dominant. It was all I wanted to be, which accounts for the six years it took me to be dragged into becoming a Switch.

On my first day of work, I came in, and who, to my wondering

eyes, appeared? Mistress Deidre… the Mistress who I first played with at the Chateau. Her eyes lit up when she saw me and claimed me as hers immediately. Remembering what I was wearing the night we met, she named me Bunny for the slippers I wore on our first encounter.

I took to my new position quickly. It was all very natural to me, and I enjoyed it. One thing that was missing was training. Sure, I was a natural submissive, but that did not mean I knew what I was doing or how to play safely. No one seemed bothered the day I did six sessions in a row in the lovely Paddles Room. There was no talk of warm-up or safe words. When I first began working, I was in a constant state of black and blue. No worry about healing before you do more sessions over the damage you already had. I did not know any better, and honestly, it did not bother me too much, but it was not very pretty.

My relationship with Deidre was complicated. Eventually, she wanted me to move in with her, which seemed like a good idea at the time, but it later became an absolute nightmare. I had a very close vanilla friend named Cindy who was protective of me and did not understand at all what the hell I was doing, but she was supportive. I was making decent money after a while and decided to give up my other job as driving from Whittier to Hollywood every day and working the two jobs became too much. Mistress Deidre had another slave with whom I became good friends; I knew him as Jim. He was

very generous to her and financed a lot of her entrepreneurial ideas. We became good friends. It turned out that he, at one time, owned one of the first BDSM clubs in Los Angeles in the '70s called Passive Arts.

Jon was great to work for. He was very kind, and I probably had a bit of a crush on him.

Mistress Patty was a character, and I was a little scared of her. She was famous for her lactating breasts. She was a Diva to the bone, and you could tell immediately that she was used to getting her way. She was not a nurturing type. I was so afraid of her! They were a lovely couple, and it was nice when they were there.

They lived in Oregon or somewhere like that, so when they were in town, it was a treat.

I also fell in love with a beautiful couple, Master Ira and Shawna. She was so sexy, and he possessed the arrogance and confidence any subby would appreciate. We had parties at Club O, and they used to perform together. What a joy to watch the two of them interact with each other. I was a bit green with envy, but I loved them both. The first time I saw hot wax done was by Master Ira on Shawna. He was dressed all in black in a Ninja-type outfit, and she was in her birthday suit (as subs usually were in those days). Every time a drop of hot wax hit her, she raised her body higher to receive it. It was just an honor to watch them.

On the homefront, things were not going well. Living with

Deidre was another abusive situation for me. I got the whole slave thing, but I was also a human being with vulnerabilities and needs as well. This is a mistake a lot of Doms make when they take a submissive. It is a give-and-take situation, not take-and-take more.

Sometimes I felt she was pimping me out because she set me up on dates with whom she thought I should be seeing. Once, she had me date a client who was a cross-dresser. He was a top but liked to dress—no problem for me. The problem was when he stole my favorite dress and would not give it back to me! The day after, when I went to work, she was angry with me that I went out with him and humiliated me in front of the entire staff by having me suck on a dildo since I liked cock so much! I am not bisexual, which created a few problems for me during my early sub years. I considered myself passive bi, which was to please the Master/Mistress. It goes hand-in-hand with being a 24/7 slave with no boundaries, I guess. Everyone needed to be happy.

One night, we had a party at Club O, and a lot of people were in attendance. I had been instructed to go down to the basement to get some firewood for the fire. As I cleared the basement door, I heard the words, "Everybody hit the floor!" A thud that shook the building came after this, and I continued downstairs in a panic, not knowing what the hell to do. I was terrified. I found a closet and hid inside for what seemed forever. I heard doors slamming and, finally, people talking. I could not move; I was frozen with fear inside the

closet. Next, I heard a ticking sound in the closet, so of course I thought there was a bomb in the building, and I still could not move! I was too scared to speak or even cry. I was barely breathing. I heard footsteps coming down the stairs, and my heart raced.

I had been found. Thankfully, it was one of the ladies who had been told to find me. Once she pried me out of the closet and helped me upstairs, I found out we had been robbed. Luckily, some of the ladies escaped the building in their lingerie and were able to call the police. The officers were genuinely nice, to my surprise. I was not sure how they would take to us, but cops see it all, don't they? Obviously, I had nothing to contribute to the conversation, so I just stayed close to everybody and was happy to go home that night. My angel was with me again.

To my surprise, I wanted to go back to work. I really loved it there. Most of the ladies were friendly, and I loved doing my sessions. I felt like I was on the road to getting my kids back sooner with the money I was making. One day, Jon called me into his office and said he had an offer for me. He wanted to take me to Oregon with him and Mistress Patty. I was so flattered, but I just couldn't. Now Carl, I think, considered himself a Master/Mentor to me, although there was no official relationship. There seemed to be some friction between himself and Jon about this (so I was told). Carl and Jon had a falling out, and since the lease was in Carl's name and the landlord decided we were running a "whorehouse," we needed to leave. This was so sad. It was the most beautiful place I ever worked

and the perfect BDSM venue. Club O had to go.

There was still the matter of Mistress Deidre looming in the background. Day by day, things just got worse. I had the flu one day and stayed home from work. She came in late, and her ex-husband stopped by. He was nice. She wanted me to get out of my sick bed and walk to the store in the rain to get food and then cook him a meal. He was embarrassed and insisted it was not necessary. Because I hesitated, she became irate and started screaming at me, and I decided that it wasn't for me. I left, and I went to my friend's house. My friend Cindy always supported me but was not a fan of Deidre. I called Deidre the next day to let her know I would be coming by to pick up my things that day and was told I had nothing to pick up. Arrrrrrggggghhhhhh!!!!!! Cindy drove me there, and we ended up calling the cops for help getting my things. Deidre, of course, told them everything in the house was hers. She was ranting and a little crazy! This was getting ugly. The apartment was on the second floor. I quickly grabbed my things, and then the argument over the TV started. The police let me take my TV, and she lost it. As I was walking down the stairs and into the courtyard, she was yelling over the railing that I would never see my kids again. Of course, the neighbors were all out to see what the kerfuffle was. She was yelling that I was a slave and trying to humiliate me publicly. Thank God to my friend Cindy, who helped me keep it together and got me out of there. I don't know that I would have done it without her.

Going to a residential area in La Habra was not one of the best moves ever for a BDSM club, but that is where we ended up. It seemed so remote after being in Hollywood. Business was slow, and eventually, the Club folded. All in all, Club O was a great experience for me, and I felt lucky to have worked there.

I worked with a lovely lady named Chiffon, who decided to open a club of her own in North Hollywood called the Villa. She invited me to work with her, and I was happy to do so. The club was a work in progress, and it was not busy. It was also a long drive for me to get there. I stuck with her for as long as I could, and then I found out about Lady Laura's Dominion. It was in the Beverly-Fairfax area in Los Angeles, which was a better drive for me. I called and asked about work and was invited to come in for an interview. I was so nervous. I had heard so many things about Lady Laura, and there were mixed reviews of her.

# LADY LAURA'S DOMINION

I wanted to look my best, so I dressed in my finest outfit and went to meet her. I was on time, of course, as any good submissive would be. I was surprised to find that Lady Laura's was two blocks away from the original Club O, where I started. I parked my car, walked up to the door, and rang the bell. There was a small porch you entered when you went in with black-and-white tile floors that made a great sound under my heels. There was a step up into the house, and the desk was right at the door, and there she was in all her splendor. The light from the desk gave an added glow to an already dazzling sight. She wore spandex pants with a loose-fitting shirt and boots. Her fingernails were long, and several big gold chunky rings adorned her fingers. Her makeup was impeccable, and her hair teased as high as it could go in typical '80s fashion. On her lap was a beautiful white cat who I later found out was part of a trio going by the names Gucci Gumdrops, Tiffany Tears, and Cinders. Those cats ruled!

When Lady Laura greeted me, she did so with a hug, which caught me off guard and made me love her instantly. With cigarette in hand, Bette Davis style, she showed me around her home-slash-dungeon. To the right of the desk was the living room. The house had an art-deco theme. She favored the color dusty rose. A few ladies were sitting on the big, curvy couch watching the biggest TV

I had ever seen. There was a stone fireplace, and it was all very cozy. Walking to the back of the house, there were two rooms. One was the Red Room, and the other the Blue Room. Each had suspension, bondage tables, and a spanking horse. The bathroom was large with two sinks, which came in handy for all the ladies working. Then she took me through her bedroom, which had an enormous four-poster bed. I was told this was her room and that no sessions were done there. We walked through the bedroom to the back door, which led to a garage. You had to dodge the two dogs to get to the garage, which was kind of scary and funny at the same time. The garage was an amazing dungeon. It was large and had a jail cell and, of course, a bondage table and a spanking horse. I loved this room… it was a fantasy room.

After the tour, we talked. I gave her my history, and she told me the rules of the house. She also talked to me about safety, which was a first and really put me at ease. I felt at home with her, and I felt connected to her. She made me feel safe. We talked about advertising. This was before the Internet, of course, and advertising was all printed in the local adult newspapers. It was kind of nice that BDSM was harder to find back then. The clients that came in had really searched and, for the most part, were very appreciative and pretty good players. If I correctly recall our rates, they were $120 an hour, and it was a 55/45 split. The ladies were getting 45 percent plus tips. For me, this was good money, and I was very happy to have the opportunity to be a part of Lady Laura's Dominion.

I was super submissive. I knew how to act and how to dress, I knew the submissive protocol, and I would not say mercy! I was a natural, and I learned that I was damned special. I was not the prettiest, the thinnest, or the sexiest, but I was real, and clients who saw me appreciated that. I loved the attention, and I felt valued. I was living the dream. I was a BDSM baby who had found her home, and I had a lot to learn. I trusted everyone who came in, but it eventually became a mistake and downright stupid. I was living in my fantasy world where I was the cool girl, but the reality was I was bought and paid for and, at times, treated like dirt by clients. Because I was not the prettiest, it was okay to beat the shit out of me. While I was taught to say mercy, my stubborn nature did not allow me to use it. Once I hit my stride, I developed a reputation for being a heavy submissive, and there were days when all I did were several heavy sessions in a row. In those days, that did not translate to dollars as it does now. It was plain stupid in retrospect.

God Bless the Ladies I worked with. I was a source of constant frustration to them for my lack of self-worth. They were so supportive of me when I had a bad session and would talk to me and teach me things I needed to know. Switch Bree was someone who taught me economics. It makes no sense to let someone hurt you so severely for the same amount of money someone getting tickled is making. Simple, right? I always felt that if I earned it, I would get it, but that was not the case. Bree took the cane a lot but also demanded a $100 fee for taking it. Eventually, I did get up the nerve

to do this, and it was a massive part of my growth as a submissive: learning self-worth.

The most interesting place in Lady Laura's was the bathroom. This is where the Ladies got dressed, gossiped, and did drugs. Lady Laura called it '*the Densa meeting in the bathroom.*' Cocaine was a huge part of the BDSM culture back then in the '80s, and a few ladies were hooked on heroin as well.

While not everyone partook in drugs, a lot did. I was kind of a submissive snob because I felt that the ladies using coke were cheating when it came to taking pain. I was a purist and could do it with no help. I had never taken a drug in my life, nor did I smoke until I started working in the clubs. Clients who used to frequent Lady Laura's will remember the cloud of smoke hovering in the rooms because so many of us smoked back then. Drugs were commonplace for the clients who came in, too. No one really minded if a client was doing cocaine because he would usually do long sessions. We used to work until the clients stopped coming in, sometimes into the wee hours of the morning.

I will admit that I had a brief encounter with cocaine myself. It began for me because the ladies doing it swore by it for weight loss. Well, for me that was all I had to hear. It was effortless to get because the ladies that used it had easy access to it and were dealing as well as using it. I pretty much started slow, and I never got hooked; just got stupid. I did lose weight, but I was more into the

energy I had using it. I only used it for a matter of months. I have mentioned a couple of times that I believe someone has always looked out for me, and this was one of those times. One night, I went out with one of the ladies, and we met at a strip club in the Valley called Filthy McNasty's. I left the club and got into my 1971 Pinto, which was not only a dangerous car to drive but also bad for the environment. When I drove it, the exhaust that came out of the back was so bad someone reported me to the EPA! I was leaving the club and made a U-turn, and the next thing I knew, police lights were flashing in my rear-view mirror. Oh shit!

Stupid me had a vial of coke in the console of the car, and I was in a panic. I pulled over and got out of the car, and I am sure I was obviously tweaked. The officer looked into my eyes and then told me to walk in a straight line. Please keep in mind here that I was wearing a white leather outfit with six-inch stilettos with silver tips. I asked if I could take my shoes off and was told no, so I was sure they were having a bit of fun with me. I did the impossible walk, and the officer looked at me and, God Bless him, he asked me how old I was, and I told him. He told me that night that if I did not stop, I would not live to see my next birthday, and he let me off with a warning and sent me home. This truly shook me up, and one would think that that would have been enough for me. I just became more careful. I went out one night with one of the ladies, and we stopped at my house. The details are blurry as to what was going on, but the experience has been seared in my mind for life. I am 100 percent

sure I had taken too much that day because I thought I was going to die. I was lucky the person I was with knew how to deal with me. I don't know what was going on physically, only what was in my head. My daughter was asleep in the room next to mine, and I remember thinking the entire time I cannot do this to my daughter. I saw the light that night, and I heard people speaking in tongues, and I was sure I was going to die, but I kept thinking about my daughter, and I kept coming back to her while feeling so much shame. The lady who was with me had a gallon container of water and just kept making me drink and talked to me the whole time. I don't really know how bad the situation was; I only know how I felt. I think she would have taken me to the hospital if I was overdosing, but who knows? I only know I was grateful to her. That is what made me stop. It was very easy for me after that. My kids always snapped me back from being an idiot. I still carry the shame in my heart for this, but I did learn, and I am always grateful for the help of my friend and for learning the lesson.

Going to work was like going home to my second family. There was such a sisterhood back then.

It was a different time. There were not so many ladies working, and most of the Ladies working were into BDSM and sought it out for that reason. As I've previously mentioned, there was no Internet, and we advertised it in the local adult papers and Free Press. It was not easy to find us, and if you did, you were sincere about it. Most of the clients were really into BDSM and took the time to learn how

to use the equipment.

One afternoon, a beautiful Asian man walked into The Dominion. He was dressed to the nines in a black shirt with silver tips on the collar, black pants, and, of course, boots with silver tips. His hair was in a pompadour. He was very sexy, and – lucky me! – I was the submissive he wanted to see. He wanted to do a long session, and I was to be a prisoner of war. This session was very intense and emotionally draining. There was a lot of interrogation, which he excelled at, and of course, there was the punishment incurred for not giving up secrets. I remember feeling disturbed by it because it seemed so natural for him. But I was not frightened; I thought it was therapeutic for him in some way. It was a beautiful scene, and I was honored to have been chosen to play out this fantasy with him.

BDSM professionals are not given the credit they deserve for helping people work out some things that are confusing and sometimes tragic for them. Just being able to play out a situation and not be judged or asked questions is very freeing to some people. These memories are treasures to me when I can think back to someone and know I made a difference in their life.

# SUBMISSIVE AND STUPID

One night, I went out with some friends to a swingers club, and

I met a man named Alex who ticked all the boxes. I was lying on a bed, and he just appeared out of nowhere. He seemed to have a light surrounding him. He reached down and pulled me up by the hair. I loved it! I was being taken! Later, that would become a more accurate statement than I care to admit. I left with him, and we drove around LA in the early morning hours and just talked. He seemed perfect. He was a photographer and musician, attended Harvard, was handsome, sexy as hell, and very dominant. He took me to his studio in Hollywood and told me I would be staying there, and when he wanted me, he would come to me. I am sure this seems like a bad idea, but it never crossed my mind at the time. It was all too exciting. He left, and I was locked in the studio. I had no idea where I was, and there were no phones.

I acquainted myself with the studio. It seemed run down to me and not what I envisioned a successful photographer's studio to look like. I think he was just messy. Costumes were hanging, props here and there, and a bed and a bathroom. I thought to myself that I was obviously not the first woman he had brought here. Later in the day, he appeared with some food for me, used me, and left. The next day, he came again with food and an announcement that I would be quitting my job at the denim store and moving out of my cute little apartment in Whittier and I would be moving into the studio. When I had proved to him that I was a good and loyal submissive, I would be given house privileges. I don't remember hesitating for a minute… in my mind, this all seemed too wonderful to imagine.

I did have responsibilities in life I needed to attend to, and most importantly, I had children. They were still with their father, but I felt I was headed in the right direction to get them back with me, and having a partner would make that day come sooner rather than later. I had a lot of time to think when I was alone in the studio. I was allowed to go to work at Lady Laura's. That was where the money was, of course.

I gave notice at my apartment, moved all my things into storage, and wrapped up that chapter of my life, looking forward to a better one.

To me, my relationship seemed so magical, and I thought I was truly living my fantasy. I think a lot of subs have the 24/7 dream. What I did not know about my magical relationship was there was more to this than I was aware of. I felt so proud when my "Master" dropped me off at work and picked me up. I loved having to ask permission to do anything, and I had no problem giving this man every dime I made and getting an allowance. He was going to take care of me and make sure all my bills got paid. I mean, that is what I would have done as a Mistress. It is supposed to be a two-way street. I was a treasure in my mind and should be treated as such. Eventually, I was moved out of the studio and into his home. I was so excited to see the room I would be sleeping in.

Did he have a dungeon in his house? What was the kitchen like? Where did he live? Well… the nightmare begins. I was taken to a

tiny rundown apartment in Hollywood on Hollywood Boulevard and Kingsley Street. This was not one of the finer neighborhoods in Los Angeles, but I had been penniless most of my adult life and was always able to make wherever I lived nice and homey, and I was content. So I felt this could happen here with a bit of elbow grease and perhaps a bed in my room. This was not the best part. The best part came when I met his twin daughters and his "cousin," who lived with him in this ridiculously small apartment. My bubble was burst, BUT I was a real submissive and knew I could please him. His cousin took care of the twins, but I don't think she did much with the house, and I know he did nothing.

Lady Laura was not thrilled with my situation, and thus, the words "Submissive is not stupid" became a daily mantra to me from her. I was in love and knew I could make a difference to him and make him happy, and I was a slave. What could I do? I don't know when the last day this man had worked was nor where he got his money, but he smoked pot like there was no tomorrow. I hated riding in the car with him once I figured out he was constantly stoned. I was very uncomfortable in his home and probably immediately knew that it would not work out, but I always kept my commitments. I was accustomed to abuse; this was just a new flavor.

Once he figured out I was a money machine, he started dropping me off at Lady Laura's for days at a time, which turned into a week at a time, and when he needed money, he just came by and picked it

up and left me there. This was when depression and self-worth issues came to the forefront of my mind. I felt Laura was always disappointed in me during this time, and she encouraged me constantly to leave him. I was never going to get my kids back at this rate. I don't recall how long I stayed with him, but I know it was more than a year. I used to feel so grateful when he would pick me up on Sundays and take me to a cheap motel for a mercy fuck. This is when he started to give me cocaine because I was a good girl. It was a blessing, and I guess I only saw him on Sundays. He began to bring strange women, whom I presumed he picked up off the street, to join us. A lot of the time, he would just watch. He knew I was humiliated by this and derived great pleasure from it. The relationship between us, in reality, became sort of a pimp/ho type, I think. Everything was about money. It took me a long time, but I was seeing that I was once again in an abusive relationship and needed to do something about it.

I looked forward to staying at Laura's after a while and needed to figure out how the hell to get out of this situation. I needed something out of my storage one day and had a day off, so my friend drove me to my storage to find all my things had been auctioned off due to nonpayment. This was something Alex was supposed to take care of—the one thing that was important to me. I lost everything I owned, but the worst of it was all my children's things were gone, and these things were irreplaceable.

That was it for me. Laura had told me many times, "Leave the

bastard … he is just using you," and she, of course, was right. On this day, I went to his apartment to pick up a few belongings. I did not have much. I just wanted to get out as quickly as possible while no one was home. I grabbed the pictures of my kids and a small bag of my things, got out of the house, and started walking down the street to the bus stop. Unfortunately, he saw me get out of his car and grabbed me. He yanked the pictures out of my hands and threw them to the ground, shattering the glass in all of them. He threw me to the ground, and some neighbors interceded so I could get away. Two hours later, I made it to Laura's on the bus. When she saw me, she asked what was wrong, and I told her the whole story. I thought she would be so proud of me, but she was angry that I left. I was baffled because all this time, she had been telling me to leave him, and now that I had, she was pissed. She told me that I had to go back! It seems that in those days, the easiest way to get a club closed was to have a lady with a pissed-off boyfriend. Things were so underground and hidden that a mad boyfriend calling the cops was a frequent occurrence, and she did not want this to happen to her club. So, I went back. I groveled, begged for forgiveness, and was punished.

My mind had snapped into a huge reality check by now. I was on my own with no help.

During this time, my daughter was having problems with her dad. She called me and wanted to leave her father and come to stay

with me. She was 15 at the time. I was so worried about bringing her into my situation, but I had no choice but to do my best. I just wanted to get her to me, and I knew everything would fall into place. I was mortified to take her into this house. I slept on a mattress in a small room, and the place was nasty. There was nothing I could do quickly to change things. We stayed no more than a couple of weeks, and I just could not take it anymore.

So, sometimes being submissive is stupid, but fortunately, I survived the whole mess and was able to pick myself back up and move on. I view this now as part of the growing-up process one goes through when being a newbie. The trick is to learn from it! I have told this story to countless subbies in my life as a warning to them and to teach them the value they have as a submissive and a human being.

This was my daughter, my life, and she deserved better. We packed up, and I moved into a motel with my daughter near Laura's, and within a month, we had our own place. It was great, just the two of us in our girly apartment with nothing in it. The first thing I bought was a bed for her, and we had a beautiful Christmas that year with our white tree and pink trimmings. We had nothing, but we had each other, and it was good. I was back in Mommy mode, which is where I always do my best and strongest.

I was still making decent money and could start working on getting my boys back with me now. It did not take me long to get

my sons back with me as I worked seven days a week and did so most of the time that I had my kids. I was so happy to have all my kids back with me. Any single mother will tell you how difficult it is to balance working and taking care of your kids. At this time, my kids were teenagers, so it was a little easier to leave them to go to work. Like any mother in my situation, I did my best, which was not always enough. Spending time with your teen children is essential. I was lucky because my kids were able to talk to me. They told me everything or everything they wanted me to know. Overall, they were good kids. There were some issues during high school, but all my children grew to be successful in their chosen fields and were good parents. I am proud of all of them.

# TEACHERS

One of the many blessings of being a BDSM baby at this time was the amazing women I was surrounded by daily. They were all characters, as was I and I was able to study my craft with some fantastic women and mentors. I grew up with the likes of Mistress Tantala, who was a porn star as well as a Domina. She was very intimidating and was a Master of Fantasy and roleplay. Her verbal skills were incredible, and I marveled at her confidence and ability to spin a fantasy so well you were right there in the middle of it.

Back in those days, we all loved multiple lady sessions, which were fun for everyone. One of my favorites was a scene with Mistress Tantala, who was the warden in a prison. There were two other ladies, plus the client. We were in the dungeon garage, complete with guard dogs outside should we attempt to escape. Now, anyone who knew me when I was a submissive knew that I loved getting under Dom's skin or starting trouble with the other subs. I was great at getting the other subs in trouble, especially the male subs, because I always looked so innocent. Cheering Mistress Tantala on while she punished the male sub in the room was great fun. There was only one cage, so we were locked in the cage and taken out one by one until we were strung up all over the room. Because I had a high pain tolerance, I so enjoyed it when the Dom made threats to get me to do something I did not want to do and

made threats. I was of the mindset of "Give it your best shot; I won't break!" While this was a serious scene, we all ended up laughing 'til we cried. We had so much fun with each other, and the client had a very unforgettable time.

There was also Mistress Holly, who was a strict disciplinarian with a British accent. She was a very kind lady who was going through some child custody issues because of the work she was doing. I saw so much of this in the scene, and it still goes on today. Sex workers were under constant threat of being "outed" by ex-partners. This put them in danger of losing their children, other jobs, or their homes. In fact, I had to pay off my former Master to leave me and The Dominion alone.

One of my favorite teachers was Mistress Jacqueline. She was a video star and an amazing Dom, standing less than five feet tall. She used to take me into her sessions and let me train on some of her clients. I was enthralled at the command she took of a room despite her small frame. She was a great example of a powerful woman and dispelled some stereotypes at the same time.

There was Mistress Pamela who, when she was bored, lit candles on the fireplace and put them out with a bullwhip. She was very into yoga and earthy things. Pamela was charming and very nurturing. She was more of a sensual Domina and spoke very softly and precisely in a session.

Who can forget Mistress Rachel, the beautiful Australian who

could do more sessions in a half-hour than anyone I ever met? Rachel had a great sense of humor and was very creative when it came to humiliation. I remember a day coming in, and she had a crossdresser decked out in the finest leather slithering across the floors. He could not do anything else because he was tied up from head to toe, including a leather hood. I admired her so. She was such a beauty and had that great accent. The guys would do anything for her. She was and still is a legend.

Mistress Valkyrie was a tall woman of German descent with long, waist-length blonde hair. She taught me to pierce one of her slaves. I was so scared. Her slave started taunting me, calling me a pussy, which inspired me to stick the needle in his balls like he was a pin cushion. It was exhilarating. Piercing became one of my favorite things to do, and I made my own kit and had sterile needles supplied to me by a nurse-client of mine. I took it very seriously and was so proud when I could pierce and not draw a drop of blood. She was a great teacher who became a good friend to me and helped me a lot during our time together.

Lady Kalleen Hillier, the 6'3" Amazon, was married to Sir James at one time, and she started the Chateau with him. When she entered the room, she was the room! She had lots of stories, and she loved sharing them. We used to joke around with her that she just tied up her clients, and the torture was talking to them until they said mercy. Kalleen was very generous with her time, teaching me and sharing sessions as well to help me learn. She also introduced me to

beautiful music. She knew a lot about classical music and introduced me to New Age music, which I still enjoy listening to to this day.

Lady Olivia Outré was a great friend of mine. She was the youngest Dom in Los Angeles when she began her career. She was a talented rope rigger and in great demand for bondage videos. She is a petite fiery redhead who knows her stuff and puts up with no crap. She was super creative in session and used to like having Ladies join her in session to help teach them. There was a problem with this one day when one of the Ladies came down from her cameo to tell everyone that Olivia had stuck a Big Stick somewhere the sun didn't shine and how cool it was. We are talking about "the Popsicle" here. I didn't care, but we had a strict policy of no penetration, so I had to take her to the side to talk to her about it. I loved the idea of it, and basically, don't bring the kids in if you are sticking something up someone's ass.

Two consenting adults it was not a big deal to me, but if one does, all do. These are just a few, and I am sure I have forgotten some, and my apologies for that. These Ladies were legendary, and I was honored to be able to learn from them.

I did a lot of reading on the subject of BDSM and bought every book I could on the topic to learn as much as I could, but I promise you that learning on the job was the best teacher. You learn how to do things and how NOT to do things in session when you are new. When you finally do become a Dom or Switch, you remember not

to wrap someone with a flogger (which is hitting them so the thongs of the flogger wrap around the body and speed up, leaving marks). You remember to hold a candle high when dripping candle wax on someone's body until you are sure that they are comfortable with the heat of it.

I had my own idea of what a submissive should be. I was accommodating and pleasant, treated my clients like they were kings, and remembered what they wanted when they returned to see me. I was stoic in my sessions, and when I was being punished, I never uttered a sound. That was my idea of what a submissive should be. About three years into submission, I accidentally made a noise in session with someone I had seen repeatedly, and he was thrilled! He commented on how exciting it was that I made noise. We talked about it after the session was over and how much more satisfying the scene was for him with the response. From that day forward, I responded in my sessions unless instructed to do otherwise.

I never knew how many other fetishes existed when I started. The first time I did a food session, I was flabbergasted and did not get it. The session went like this... The client had a selection of shoes in the room, and I put a pair on. I walked around the room and then out of the room. Went back into the room and changed shoes, repeating this process until all the shoes had been worn. Then, I was told to go into the shower, where he produced chocolate syrup, molasses, honey, and eggs. He poured the sticky stuff over my head and let it drip down my body, and then put the eggs in my bra and

smashed them with his hands. He said thank you and left the room. That was it. There are countless types of food sessions, including the pie in the face or your butt in the pie. One client came in regularly to have baked beans put down his pants, and he always brought his own beans. The messiest sessions usually involved a tarp because it was a free-for-all of every messy kind of food you can imagine, all over both parties and lots of times not all on the tarp. Sadly, we had to stop doing food sessions because the cleanups were not always as thorough as I would have liked them to be, and ants in the building have not been a fetish request that I have ever heard of yet. I am sure it is out there, though!

While tickling is a big thing now, there were not a lot of tickle sessions during my time. There was one client who came in and tickled and recorded the laughter so he could play it over and over when he went home. He was very particular about his feathers as well. I respected tickling sessions but thought they were better saved for the girls who couldn't take it. Most ticklers were a lot of fun, but then there was the tickle torture – the guys who dug their fingers into your ribs and caused pain. They were found out in pretty short order, and not a lot of people wanted to play with them.

The day-to-day outside of sessions in the house was always interesting. We were able to leave and go up to Beverly Boulevard and do a bit of shopping between sessions or get some lunch and bring it back. It was like a big, long, glorious pajama party most of

the time. I think we all genuinely cared for each other. I knew we had each other's backs by the way we looked after each other during sessions, listening at the doors if we heard the wrong noise, warning each other about clients we had a nasty session with, and the simple girly things we did together when filling time.

Some of the best times were listening to Lady Laura's stories of her escapades. She was a beautiful woman who resembled Angie Dickinson in her younger years. She was a swinger who used to go to the infamous A-Frame in the Hollywood Hills. The infamous porn star John Holmes who was famous for the size of his dick, was like a brother to her, and she would tell us about the times she would hold his dick in both of her hands and just how heavy it was. She was Miss Nude USA and parachuted out of an airplane in the buff, and she was very proud of her "rose bush." (Figure it out!)

Lady Laura began her career at the Chateau with Sir James. The story was that she and James did not get on too famously because she refused to call him Sir. She liked to taunt him and call him Jimmy. To be fair, I have heard other versions of this story, but this is the one I like best. Lady Laura left the Chateau and started working out of her own place on Curson Avenue in West Hollywood. Later, she bought a house in Edinburgh, where I began working with her.

The house was great. It was comfortable for the Ladies and the clients. Clients, of course, came from all over the world, and some

of our faves used to cook for us in the kitchen. I think Chicken Soup Richard was the most loved. He used to bring in huge duffle bags of beautiful lingerie he had dyed in lovely colors and stockings to sell to us at a reasonable price. This was another cool thing about this time. While there were not a lot of places to buy clothing for our work, we had a lot of people bring the clothing to us, and we could shop while working. Lots of equipment-makers brought equipment to us to sell as well. It was always a nice break in the day, and it felt like Christmas when they came by.

Of course, Lady Laura had her work cut out for her. I doubt there was anything she did not know about all of us, and she was patient and caring as well. Occasionally, the kids would get rowdy, though, and these were great times. One day, while she was answering phones, Mistress Rachel was in session with an exhibitionist. He wore spandex that showed every curve and point in his body to get to The Dominion, and once he was there, Mistress Rachel would just let him loose in the house.

That day, Laura was talking to her mom on the phone, and Rachel brought her guy out into the reception area. He was a dancer (but not a professional one), and he was dancing around and flipping his source of pride up and down as he danced. He was stroking it with a stupid grin on his face, which was quite comical, and you just had to laugh while watching him. He decided to focus on Lady Laura while she was on the phone. As he danced around her, she waved

him away, which made it even more exciting for him… and the more excited he got, the happier he got. She would turn away from him, and he would dance to the other side.

At this point, we were all rolling because it was the funniest sight. We did not realize Laura was getting pissed, but I don't think we could have helped ourselves even if we did. Besides, he was not our client; he was Rachel's. Eventually, Lady Laura got off the phone, gave him hell, and shooed him back to a room where he finished his dance privately. She was good about it and ended up laughing, too.

There were so many good times with good friends' clients who genuinely cared about you and became friends as well. There were also dangerous times and evil clients. Lady Laura was not well-liked by the male club owners, which caused problems on occasion. They felt that all women were slaves and had no business running a club, so they did their best to make Laura's life difficult.

Lady Laura was very friendly, and the clients loved her. This made her place very popular, and we had a great clientele. The men who ran the other clubs were regularly making threats toward us. Some threatened to report us to the city for zoning violations, while others vowed to send people in to throw acid on the Ladies' faces in session. This is about the time that I began learning that the BDSM community was not much different than life in the real world. There were assholes everywhere.

As a submissive, I had some terrifying sessions as well. One day, I went into the Red Room with a client after our interview, where we discussed a pretty straightforward session, with some spanking and a little humiliation—it seemed fine to me. As soon as we were in the room, he grabbed me and threw me against the wall, pulled a bungee cord out of his pocket, and put it around my neck. I froze; I could not speak, and that turned out to be the entire session. I did not utter a sound for the entire 30 minutes…

First, because I couldn't make myself do it and also because I was worried that if I did not just go along with it, he would hurt the Ladies outside. I was convinced he was going to kill us all. Fortunately, he was just a crazy motherfucker, and he left with me in the room, shattered and shaking. Laura came to check on me, and I told her what happened. She was sympathetic but aggravated at the same time. Why would I let someone do that to me? I still don't know to this day.

One night, a man came in wearing a ski mask. I don't know if Laura knew who he was, but for some reason, I ended up in a session with him with no interview, and again, I felt that the end was nearly half an hour long.

Being a heavy submissive was a source of pride for me but also a challenge to others who just wanted to get me to say mercy. I did some insanely intense sessions. I could take alligator clips on my nipples, which seemed to be a client favorite for me. I used to love

it when the ladies got big tips or lovely gifts from the clients, and I got nipple clamps. It became comical to me as time went on but was also a source of sadness for me. I did a session once where the client ripped the alligator clamps off my nipples, and they bled.

Two days later, I noticed red lines on my breast and showed Lady Laura, who took me to the doctor. I had blood poisoning. A client I had been seeing for a while came to visit. He was doing his last session ever and wanted to use the dungeon outside. We knew him, so Lady Laura okayed it. We went outside, and he tied me to a table and told me he was going to rape me. Terror! He did not, but he did leave an impression on me for some time with the burns on my breasts from using birthday candles for wax play and holding them as close as possible to my skin. My poor boobies were blistered and scarred for some time. I felt blessed that no permanent scarring had occurred.

I always felt I should be able to trust the women I worked with, but, just like in life, that is not always the case. One example of this was a session with a Mistress whom I considered a friend. She had been offered a large tip to get me to mercy in a session. She was given only thirty strokes with the implement of her choice. She chose a homemade whip that was pure evil. It was made from an ax handle and had about twenty-three-foot-long thongs similar to boot laces. I never discussed limits with the Dommes I worked with, simply because I felt safe with them. But money seems to be an impetus to throw out the rule book sometimes, and things can get

messy.

I was spread-eagled, hanging from the suspension bar. The client was sitting across from me in a chair, and all he wanted to do was watch me break. When the first strike hit, I knew I was in trouble. The Mistress either did not know how to use this whip properly or was deliberately wrapping it around my hips to intensify the pain and the damage.

I had already made up my mind before going into this session that I would be winning this battle, no matter the price. She carried on delivering each badly-aimed blow, continuing to wrap me with each one. I could feel her getting more frustrated every time she swung the whip. The client sitting in the chair was egging her on and cheering for her to hit me harder. Yes, it hurt! It was brutal! We reached 15 strokes, which was the magic number for me—the halfway point.

I was past the point of mercy, and it would never happen now. She got angry with me and started yelling at me and calling me names as she whipped me. She was furious and out of control, and as far as I was concerned, once a Domme loses her cool, she loses all respect. All she could see were hundred-dollar bills flying out of her reach every time she hit me. 30! I did it! I won! Fuck you both!

She did not get her tip, and, of course, I did not get one either. Why would I? Lady Laura was pissed when she saw my side. It was more than just marked. Those lumpy black and blue bruises… a

badge of honor for my victory!

Over the years, it became my great joy to piss off the female Dommes. The better a submissive I became, I felt emboldened to spice up the sessions and make them more interesting by exploiting the weaknesses of the Dommes. Most were very good sports about it and enjoyed the sessions as much as I did. The clients liked it, and whatever the consequences were for my bad behavior, I could take them.

Once I figured this all out, I felt empowered in my sessions. Whenever a "Master" wanted things that were not agreed on in our interview or pushed for sexual favors and threatened me with punishment, it became a "go for it" situation. I knew there was nothing they could do to me that would make me change my mind, and I was ready, willing, and able to take the punishments they used to threaten me to get their way. The combination of my stubbornness and high pain tolerance made me very sure of a personal victory by the end of the session. They would leave without the sexual favors they thought they could beat out of me, and I had a nice warm ass. I am 'No Mercy Bunny!'

Sometimes couples would come in and play which was fun a lot of times. One time, a lady and her partner came in. She was a wrestler named Nancy. We weren't going to wrestle, but I knew her from being in the scene. So, a female sub in a room with a female Domme would probably feel pretty safe, right? Not in this case. This

woman was a straight-up bitch. She was mean and sadistic with no style. And she didn't know how to use the equipment, which is a bad thing for someone who seems to have anger issues. That's what I felt in the room with her.

She hated me for some reason and was going to make me feel as bad as she possibly could, both physically and mentally. This was the first time in my life anyone had ever spit on me. I cried, but I would never give her the satisfaction of a mercy. Once the session ended and she left, Lady Laura drew me a bubble bath and brought me a glass of wine so I could soak and cry in the bathroom for a while. It was a very sweet moment between us because I could feel she cared for me, and I felt safe again.

Lady Laura and I had such a beautiful connection. My children loved her and called her "Other Mother." She was very good to me most of the time, and I knew she loved me. I became her submissive without ceremony. It was just a given. We did not have a sexual relationship, which was a disappointment to those with overactive imaginations. It was more of a mother/daughter love.

One day, I was sitting in the living room, and a Master and his submissive came through the door. She was adorable—a tiny little thing with dark curly hair and dark eyes. Her Master seemed very kind and proud of her. She was going to join Lady Laura's, and this would lead to a lifelong friendship for us. Her name was Gina. She was a true submissive, and I was a little envious of her as she seemed

to have it all: looks, intelligence, a sweet nature, and a tattoo on her ass that said "precious slave." This tattoo struck me as one of the most beautiful things I had seen in a long time. I imagined the thought behind it for both her and her Master and the pride she had in wearing his mark.

I instantly adored her but envied her at the same time. We developed a beautiful friendship eventually and, at the same time, became very competitive in sessions. A double session with Gina and Bunny was a wonder. We both fed off of each other during the session, and she delighted in getting me in trouble as much as I did her. One of my most memorable times with her was at an "O Party" in Big Bear that she and her Master took me to for the weekend. This was my first BDSM weekend, and I was ready. It was put on by Scorpio, which is a small group of Male Doms and female subs. This was a fantasy come true—a weekend in the woods with a bunch of like-minded people!

I belonged to her Master that weekend, but he was generous with letting me play with others. The thing I wanted most out of the weekend was to get tied to a tree somehow and flogged! The event was in a big ski lodge with lots of rooms and a huge common area as well. We were in service the entire weekend, which was totally my thing, and I loved every minute of it. There were submissive games in which, depending on your state of mind, losing could be a big win!

I remember the obstacle course. There was a huge tarp laid out on the floor, and we had to lie on it blindfolded, which I gladly did. I lay there, and suddenly, I felt this warm liquid all over my body. It was so comforting and sexy. I was not sure what it was as I had never experienced hot wax before. It turned out that several pillar candles had been burning in glass for hours before the course, which accounted for how much wax spilled on me. It was the best feeling. It was a bitch getting it all off, though. Loved it!

I met a Master at one of the play parties for whom I felt immediate respect. He was kind and seemed to be the man of the hour with a stable of slaves all to himself. His name was Lord Dan. He was flogging a lady whose arms were suspended from the ceiling. With my surrogate Master's approval, he pulled me over to him and blindfolded me. He tied my hands together, and I felt them being raised over my head while I felt the closeness of another body next to mine. It was the lady he was flogging. He continued to flog her and then me. He was very sensuous with the whip, and while this was going on, I heard in the background one of my favorite songs at the time, "Slave to Love" by Bryan Ferry.

As he continued to flog us both, the rhythm of the music became part of the scene, forcing us to writhe together with each snap of the whip. We were twisting and turning into each other, and these two strangers who just met became lovers for a moment during one of the sexiest scenes I was ever involved in publicly. Once the music

stopped, we were slowly brought down. I was in a serious sub-space and high as a kite. I had never felt anything like this before. We seemed to have made a lot of the onlookers happy as well. Lord Dan was suitably pleased and, with a peck on the forehead, sent me on my way, wanting more. Good Dom!

These were a couple of days of submissive bliss for me, and yes, I made it to the tree!

# SWITCH?

I loved being submissive. I had no aspirations of ever becoming a Domina. I was perfectly content and legendary in my position as Bunny. Once in a while I would join a session at the behest of a Dominant and just do as instructed. If she wanted me to spank someone, I did. Whatever I was told to do, I did it. I thought it was okay, but I found most of the slave boys could not take half of what I could, so I viewed them as crybabies.

Lady Laura had been encouraging me for years to become a Switch, and I just did not want to do it. I had seen enough sessions with a Domme, and I was pretty good with the equipment. I did not feel people would take me seriously as a Domme, and I lacked self-confidence in that role. I had done some Switch sessions that were not difficult, but I was not adept at bondage. Laura did not like a session walking out the door if there was no one available to see a client, and one day, my worst nightmare came to fruition. A gentleman came in and wanted to see a Domme for a bondage session. I was the only one not in session, and Laura told him he could see me. My heart sank, and my anxiety went to full force. I put him in The Red Room, closed the door, and went to talk to Laura. I told her I couldn't do it! I had never done any bondage and just knew my first bondage session was going to be a disaster. I didn't even know how to talk to him, even though I had witnessed and

experienced so many sessions as a submissive. It was not natural for me.

"Pleeeeeeaaaaassse, don't make me do it!"

"Do it," was the reply.

Oy! I was so scared. I got some rope and a blindfold, and that was it. I had no clue what I was going to do. I paced outside the room for a good 10 minutes before I got the eye from Laura. In, I went! I gave him his safe word, and the first thing I did was blindfold him. Okay, this is good… he cannot see me now or what I am doing. This is God's honest truth, and I tied him up pretty well. He felt incapacitated, which is what mattered. Had he seen the bondage, I may have lost some credibility because he had big rope bows all over him! I loved the way it looked and thought it was so silly that I called Lady Laura in to see what I had done. She smiled and gave me a thumbs-up! It was awesome, and I was very proud of myself. I was happy and the best part was the client was, too!

All our advertising was in print at this time, so we were always trying to come up with that perfect ad that would stand out from all the others. I had a great headshot of me taken where I looked very submissive and sweet. It was an eye-catcher, and the copy was addressed to "Dear Sir." Laura submitted the ad to the paper, and when the ad came out, somehow, it had become a quarter page. I was so embarrassed! My head was so big! The size of the ad did not make me look too humble. But it was perfection and caught the

attention of many new clients and one man who would become an important part of my life.

# M

M came to Lady Laura's to see me. When we met, I immediately felt that submissive excitement inside of me. He was very confident and a bit arrogant, which I was very attracted to. He had dark hair and dark eyes that I felt could see into my very soul! He was an experienced player from the Bay Area and knew exactly what he was doing.

He immediately got into my head, which was super important for me because the rest was just mechanics. If you could get inside my head, that was major, because few could figure me out, especially so quickly. He was very intense and a little dark. I enjoyed our session very much. After the session, he was aloof, and I was certain I would never see him again, but he returned the next day… and the next… and the next. I loved psychological play because it was such a great escape.

Eventually, he had to return home, but I did give him my contact information. We spoke on the phone every day. He came down to see me frequently, and then, one day, he invited me to come up to his place in Sausalito. Of course, this is breaking all of the rules. I was not much of a rule breaker, but I went for it with Lady Laura's permission. I think she was just happy for me that I had met a halfway decent human being who was interested in me.

I hate flying, but I was told to take a plane up, and he would

pick me up. Even though you are only in the air about 20 minutes from LA to San Francisco, it was terrifying for me. Some lovely woman tried distracting me with conversation and gave me a book to look at during the flight. I felt sorry for her because I was certain I was inconsolable the entire way. I made it in one piece, and he was there to get me. I had never been to San Francisco, so I was very excited to see it. He drove me around the city and showed me all the sites. Then we went to Sausalito which I just fell in love with. His place was up a hill with a long flight of steps to get up to the house. The house was nestled in the trees with a huge deck. It was a definite bachelor pad, nicely furnished but sparse—essentials only.

My first night there was an experience I will never forget. In retrospect, I have mixed feelings about my reaction at the time to the events that took place. Pleasing was my specialty, and that was all I wanted to do. He put an armchair in the middle of the room and told me to sit. I obliged, of course. I was tied to the chair and blindfolded, and he left to go to another room. When you are alone and blindfolded and tied up, every minute seems like an hour. I don't know how long he was gone, but it seemed like forever. I was in another place in my mind, so when he touched me, it scared the bejeezus out of me, which I loved. He walked around me and just talked to me. He caressed me at times and pulled my hair at other times. I never knew what to expect. Then his fingers went into my mouth and opened it slowly to tease me. Then he left, and when he returned, he put noise-canceling headphones on me, and there was

New Age music playing in my head now. I could smell marijuana, which I had never used before. He put it to my lips and told me to inhale, and I coughed, of course. One more time, and then he left.

This became a very intense meditation, which I am not very good at. I don't like being alone with myself, but eventually, my mind settled. I remember thinking to myself, "I am in San Francisco, tied up in a room alone... I just know there is going to be an earthquake!" Finally, he returned, and I felt the headphones come off and a kiss on the forehead. The blindfold was carefully removed to not pull my hair, and the ropes that bound me were untied. I was proud that I had survived this without freaking out because being alone is my least favorite thing in life. I trusted him, though, and, for all I know, he had been in the room the whole time watching me.

He made me dinner, and we spent some time outside on the deck, enjoying the trees until dark. We went back to the house, and I was pretty tired. I was allowed to shower, and when I got out, I was led back to the living room, put on the floor, and tied up. This would be where I would be sleeping that night. I had not earned the privilege of sleeping with him.

I only had a few days to visit, and one was already gone. The next day, we went around San Francisco, and he introduced me to Mr. S, one of the best makers of leather equipment and dungeon furniture. I thought I had died and gone to heaven! Just walking into the store and smelling the leather was intoxicating. When I was a

young girl, when I went shopping with my mother to places like Meijers in Michigan or a sporting goods store, I used to go right to the baseball gloves and put one on my hand and cover my face in it. The smell was intoxicating to me, even at a young age. Of course, I got in trouble, but it was worth it. Eventually, the time would come when I took great pleasure in annoying my family members with my "nasty" little habit.

M and I became an item, and I loved going back and forth to San Francisco to visit. I did learn to drive it rather than fly. It was always an adventure as he showed me the seedy side of San Francisco, which was great! I was introduced to the great Cleo Dubois and went to the Mitchell Brothers Theater. I was tied to my seat in Oracle Park during a Giants game, which was exciting and terrifying at the same time. I was so scared I was going to be found out.

He came to visit me a lot, and we continued to session at Lady Laura's. One night in January 1991, while I was working, he showed up without warning. He spoke to Lady Laura, who in turn came to me and told me to get dressed because I was leaving for the night. I was so excited. I came out to greet M, but he did not say a word to me. He took me by the hand and out to the car. I got in the car, wondering what was going on. Was I in trouble? What had I done wrong? He got in the car without a word and began driving. He was visibly upset.

The tension in the car was palpable, and the only sound was Sade's "Why Can't We Live Together" playing very loudly. He drove silently to a spot that was unrecognizable to me. He parked the car and told me to get out while he did the same. He took me by the hand and took me into a building. To this day, I don't know where I was, only that I ended up in a glass enclosure with him that I think was a sauna of sorts because it was very hot. He told me to get undressed, and I complied. It did not seem a good time to ask any questions. I was really frightened because this was an intensity I had never experienced. He directed me to turn around and spread eagle against the glass. He began to flog me with gusto.

It really hurt me emotionally because I could see he was hurting so much inside. The only words I remember were, "I hate war!" I hurt for him, but at the same time, I was happy I was able to ease his pain with my suffering. We were both drenched in sweat, and the moisture on my body made the whipping more painful. We were both children of the '60s and grew up watching the Vietnam war on television, which had impacted us both as kids, seeing the horror of it all. Once he was finished, he just hugged me. We sat on the floor holding each other and needed no words. It was a beautiful experience.

M was everything I thought I ever wanted. He inspired me and encouraged me to find myself again and rediscover things I had lost as I grew older. I used to write poetry when I was young, and I wrote a book of poetry for him which I was very proud of. I went to school

and became a paralegal while with M, which reminded me that I was not a stupid creature but actually kind of smart. I graduated second in my class.

I was not afraid of him, which was a first for me. He was kind to me, and eventually, he moved in with my children and me. He proposed to me, and we were married around 1993. He was not abusive, which was refreshing and unbelievable to me, so I was making progress in my choices. One flaw was that he was a gambler, and that was all he wanted to do. As I had already spent the first half of my life supporting the men in my life, I (in my submissive way) suggested he get a job. I needed some security, and I was certain gambling would not be offering that. He did get a job, and I appreciated that, and I did not mind that he continued to gamble.

I always preferred a submissive role in my relationships. It was just natural for me, and I felt I had struck the jackpot with M. Unfortunately, life happens, and things change. Once we got married, he began to change. I had become a Switch at work around 1988. I was strictly sub up until that point. It is kind of a natural progression in the business as you get older. What I did not expect was my status to change at home.

After we were married for a while, he slowly started teaching me things he liked having done to him but remained in his Dom role. After some time, he changed the way he spoke to me. I think the day he started calling me "Honey" was the beginning of the end. I know

that sounds weird, but his entire personality was changing, including the way he interacted with me. It turned out he was a submissive! He had been grooming me to become Dominant, which was the last thing I wanted in my relationship.

Things went on for a while, and I tried to deal with it, but it just got progressively worse for me. Submission was a physical and mental need for me. It was part of my psyche and what kept me balanced. Eventually, I talked to him and explained to him that this was not going to work for me. I could not have spelled it out better for him. I warned him if he did not change, I would leave. I gave him clear and concise details about what I needed, and he chose to ignore them. I was not happy; he had to go.

# ENTER A GIGOLO

Lady Kalleen had several slaves. One day, a smooth-talking flatterer named David came into The Dominion with her. He seemed nice enough. He told us he was an ex-cop from Kansas City. He dressed kind of like a Vegas gangster and thought he was the shit. I never got the attraction, but to each his own, I guess. Lady Kalleen was pretty serious about him – so serious, she had her name tattooed on his upper inner thigh. David threw money around like there was no tomorrow. I cannot even begin to figure out the money he spent on the most obnoxiously huge tropical flower arrangements he could find that seemed to never stop coming through the door. After a while, he and Lady Laura took a shine to each other and there he was! Lady Kalleen graciously let Lady Laura have him. (A very wise decision on her part.)

He ever so slowly became part of everyone's life at work. He was always there, which changed the work dynamic dramatically; it was a hard time. Laura was so happy to be in love and basked in it. She became a bit like the woman she did not want us to be. It was great to see her have a life outside of work, but it seemed that she was footing the bill for most everything they did. She loved going to Vegas with him where they always had their room comped. The Mirage was her favorite place to go because she loved the tigers so much. She was happy, but things were too good to be true. He started

to interfere with us like the business was his. He could not keep his hands out of the cookie jar. It made me feel a bit like he was a pimp. His macho energy was not a good mix for us. But because Lady Laura and I were so close, he bought me gifts as well to endear himself to me.

I don't remember how long they were together before a phone call came in from another Mistress in town to let Lady Laura know that he had been seeing another Dominant and buying her gifts with Lady Laura's money! This was the ultimate humiliation for Lady Laura. The kink community is small, and word gets around, so it was not long before we all knew about this and waited to see how she would handle it. She did kick him out, but not for long. He "Baby, I'm sorry-ed" himself back into her good graces, and this was a real kick in the ass to most of the Ladies who cared about her.

Lady Laura never minced words when it was about men we were with who did not treat us well or were abusive, so the way she dealt with it was shocking to us all. We were all so protective of her that it really burned our asses that he was back. He was worse than ever upon his return.

At this time, we got a notice from the zoning commission that we had to close up our shop. Our male competitors, up to their usual bullshit, had finally succeeded in getting us shut down. We were all scared for our futures, but, of course, she came through for us.

# 8875

Lady Laura had to find another home for her Dominion. This was not a simple find, for sure. Lady Kalleen told her about a lovely Tudor building on Venice Boulevard that was up for sale, and she bought it. It was not an easy buy. She had to borrow money from what amounted to a loan shark and a couple of friends to get the building, but she did it. The building was a commercial/residential property, and rooms had to be built and furnished. The downstairs was an empty shell and needed the most work. Lady Laura had a lot of help from friends and clients to get the place ready. As soon as the equipment could be moved to the new location, she was back in business. It was exciting to be moving to a new dungeon but very sad to leave the house where so many wonderful memories were made.

There was a lot to work out in the new location. The biggest thing was how not to piss off the neighbors. Discretion was important. How we pulled this off I still to this day cannot figure out, because we weren't discreet! There were outside steps to get to the top floor where the two largest dungeons were. Laura bought a bunch of black PVC long trench coats for us to wear to get up the stairs. Nothing to see here! It is perfectly normal to be wearing these coats when it is 90 degrees outside. No one would notice a thing. It still makes me smile to this day, seeing the scene in my mind's eye.

Eventually, an awning was put outside, which made things very private. One room was called *The Green Room*, which was inspired by the hunter-green carpet on the floor and the Tudor trim on the white walls. It pretty much reflected the outside of the building. There was a small kitchen and a great spiral staircase up to a small loft. The other room was called *The Rock Room*, inspired by the fake bricks painted on the wall to give it the feel of a medieval dungeon. The best part was the hole painted in the ceiling, which showed a night sky painted with fluorescent colors. It was groundbreaking at the time.

One of Laura's friends, who had been with her pretty much from the beginning, had a creative streak in him and thought it was a good idea to put black lights in the room. Great concept, except for the green teeth you had when you smiled and the fluorescent dingleberries from toilet paper remnants on asses that glowed in the dark. It was funny. People loved this room. I was always very self-conscious when bent over a spanking horse and used to check myself before sessioning in the room. It was great when you were in Domme mode, though, and wanted to humiliate someone.

Laura was very much into Art Deco, so she had the walls downstairs painted white with black trim, which later would be a very disgusting shade of yellow-brown from all the smoking that happened in that building. It was much more noticeable in the new place because it was smaller, and everyone smoked. Installing ceiling fans did nothing to alleviate the problem, and I am sure a lot

of people, especially nonsmokers, were not keen on it. Once smoking was no longer allowed in the building, clients used to joke about walking into the cloud when they came in. As smoking became more and more taboo, it became a fetish for some.

We did accommodate these sessions for as long as we could. I had a client who just wanted to be tied up while I sat on his chest and smoked for two hours. It was sickening. He was a great tipper, and it inspired me to keep seeing him. I did, however, quit smoking, and after that, there was no way I could see him. I knew if I had just one puff, I would be back to my old nasty habit.

When you walked into the building, you entered the reception area, which was small, but Lady Laura got a big black glass-top desk the size of Texas for the reception area. It was so her. The interview room was to the left of the desk and had a couch and a TV in it where we used to chill when it wasn't busy. One thing you could not do was get a session on the night "Melrose Place" was on. I wasn't into it, but it blew my mind that the Ladies would make clients wait until the show was over to even talk to them.

In the back of the building, there was The Red Room, which was much smaller than the upstairs rooms, and The Fetish Room, which was even smaller with black-and-white tile floors and a peacock chair in it for foot-fetish sessions.

It was all a good start.

Not too long after we opened, I was home, and I got a call from Lady Laura in the middle of the night telling me the building was on fire. WTF? I got in my car and drove from the Valley to find the fire department there putting out the flames. We were lucky they were so close to us and got the fire out quickly. The worst damage was smoke damage, which affected the entire downstairs area. New furniture had to be thrown out, and the walls were all charred with smoke. We still worked! We took all the furniture that was left out to the front of the building, which now had lots of plastic hung in it, and we did our best.

It was awful.

An investigation showed it was arson. Someone had made a firebomb or Molotov cocktail and threw it at the back door of the building and on the side. A suspect was found but not charged for the arson. The story of the fire somehow made it to the pages of the Wall Street Journal, which was bizarre and cool at the same time.

David and Laura's relationship became a big problem for those of us who loved her and had been around for a while. He did not have a job and spent her money quite freely with all the trips to Vegas, the jewelry, and the clothes he bought. To be fair, they bought me gifts, too, but I was running the business for her with no pay, which was not a big deal for me because I loved her, and that was just the way things evolved. Laura got me an American Express corporate card which I paid off every month. This was to help me

establish credit since I had started my young life as a woman unable to get my own credit card without my husband's approval.

We all knew what was up with David because most of us had been through something similar ourselves on some level. It is hard when you are in love to see the reality of your situation sometimes, and this was the case for Laura.

David's behavior and the way he treated the Ladies was beginning to be abusive. Around 1992, there began an exodus of staff members who were fed up with his behavior. He used to enter the building like a puffed-up peacock, inserting himself into our business like he was our pimp. The thing that drove me the craziest would be him coming in and opening up the appointment book to see how many sessions were booked for each Lady. He was inappropriate with some of the staff. He acted like:

*Lady Laura's Dominion was David's private candy shop and no longer felt female-owned and operated!*

Laura knew we were not happy with his presence, and she became very defensive about it. There was no talking to her about this. It was so sad for us to watch because she had always been the strong woman who never condoned our weakness with abusive men and always encouraged us to get out of those relationships. It was a very sad time for our BDSM family. She would not listen, so the Ladies began to leave. I am talking about The Old Guard, the Ladies who had been there and with her through all kinds of crap and had

been great and loyal supporters of Lady Laura's Dominion.

I stayed until one day when Laura came in pissed off about something and threw my American Express bill on the desk, and told me it needed to be paid. It was the first I had seen of it, and I told her so, but she was just pissed. She humiliated me in front of the staff by the way she treated me. I was her Bunny! I was so hurt. My passive "suck it up" behavior took a turn to the dark side, and I took my keys to the building and threw them on the desk, and walked out the door. I just could not watch the destruction of this legendary Lady for one more minute, and my abuse cup was full and overflowing!

*The Dominion*

*The Vault*

*Lady Laura's Lair*

*Lady Hillary's Chamber*

# THE CHATEAU

So, there I was, unemployed, with three teenagers to take care of. I needed a job! I had worked as a paralegal for two years and hated it. I found working for lawyers not to be a noble profession for me. I was way too honest and sensitive. I ended up in bankruptcy law, working for a woman I despised. I was good at my job but totally taken advantage of, since I was the one running the office and picking up her laundry. I told myself I would give it two years and see if it got better. I was miserable. I decided one day I could make more money and endure less abuse just going back to BDSM full time. I never gave it up. There was no way I could have done that because I needed it too much. So I had to find another place to play.

The obvious place to go was the Chateau, which was only blocks from my house in North Hollywood. I called Sir James, and he said he would see me. When I went in for the interview, he was very hesitant. He knew how close Laura and I were and did not know what had happened. He was a little taken aback by the situation, I think. After we spoke for some time, I convinced him of my sincerity and my loyalty to whoever I was working for. I know he was glad to have me join his staff, and it would be a vengeful feather in his cap to have me there. I came in as Submissive Bunny. The Ladies were genuinely nice to me and made me feel welcome.

It was a difficult transition for me. I loved Laura, and I loved

working for her. I felt safe there, and I was very comfortable. The Chateau was a little scary for me. First, the décor was hard on the eye. Everything was red. The layout of the rooms was a bit rough as well. There was a huge lounge for the ladies, which you walked through to get to a long hallway where all the dungeons were. There were no intercoms or safety measures in place. This did not dawn on me until one of my first sessions there. One thing to understand is that at this time, you were pretty much just told you were doing a session. There was an interview, of course, but if James said you were seeing someone, you did.

Everyone was a "friend" of James, so we were always "okay" to play with whomever. This client wanted to be in the room furthest from the lobby all the way in the back. He was a character. He was tall and lanky with a comical mustache, and he laughed a lot. He brought a radio with him to play music during the session. Today, he wanted to do bondage. Sounded simple enough. I had done a lot of breast play prior to this session, but nothing like this. He tied them so tight with a thin rope that they looked like they could burst at any moment. I was not keen on this. This is when I discovered he was not a fan of safe words. My hands were already tied behind my back, and my legs had been tied together. He then pulled down the suspension bar and attached a rope he had in place on my breasts to the suspension bar. He cranked the bar up, but my feet were still flat on the floor. Then he pulled out a handkerchief and wadded it up to put in my mouth, covering it with duct tape. Next came the

blindfold. I was terrified. I have always been claustrophobic but was able to manage it with conversation and trust in my Domme. This was not the case here.

There was no safe word available here; this was not consensual. He turned the music up on the radio as loud as it would go and cranked the suspension higher until I was pulled up by my breasts and standing on my tippy toes. I don't remember how long he may have been in the room with me, but I do remember the sound of the door slamming shut. WTF!!!! Was this a set-up, I wondered? Was I going to die like this? The time it takes to go from one end of the building to the lobby is a long time. Would someone come and check on me? Did they even know I was left in the room? I could not cry because I would choke. This was pure terror for me. Obviously, someone did come and get me eventually, but it seemed like an eternity. They got me down, and I was shaking in fear and sobbing.

Mistress Stormy helped calm me down. She was a lovely Lady and would become one of my best mentors in due time. She was pissed that it had happened. James was not sympathetic, and nothing was ever said to the client. I did take great delight the time he came back and saw someone else and thought it would be great fun to piss on an electric heater just to see what would happen. It shot him across the room. What a fucking idiot.

This ruined bondage for me, which was a shame. I was flexible and did gnarly bondage scenes as a sub, but after this incident, being

tied up made my heart race, and I began to hyperventilate. Bondage for me as a submissive was over.

I adored Mistress Stormy. She was a beautiful blonde Brit with very proper mannerisms, and I was blessed to have her take me under her wing. I had started Switching at Lady Laura's, but I was a bit of a joke to most because I was so very submissive. People did not take me seriously, and I earned the name Mistress Thumper. Stormy started sharing her sessions with me and taught me so much. One thing I credit her with was my love of ambiance in a session. None of the dungeons I had played in had music or nice lighting, which made such a dramatic difference in the way the session felt to me. Mistress Stormy had her own music and candles, and I took that with me forever.

I was not at the Chateau long before they had to change locations. Evidently, when they rented the property, they neglected to discover that a Christian book publisher was right across the street from them, and this was against zoning laws, so we had to move. Fortunately for James, the next block over offered a better space, and the move was made there. I was so happy it was not red!

I was older than most of the Ladies who worked there, so I eventually became a Dungeon Mother. I was happy to lend a sympathetic ear when needed, but there was always a lost soul who needed a little guidance.

I became a buffer between James and the Ladies, which, most

of the time, he embraced. But other times, he felt I had too much influence over them, so it was a double-edged sword for me at times. It made life simpler for him, I think; having a Dungeon Mother kept the minutia to a minimum for him. I was a problem solver, and I wanted to do my best for the place where I worked. I loved teaching the new Ladies protocol and safety, which was not something afforded to a lot of Ladies at the time. It was kind of a sink-or-swim attitude to BDSM then. Granted, there were more "lifestylers" working in the scene, but being into it and experiencing it did not always happen before you began to work professionally.

James and I got along okay. I genuinely liked him. He seemed to be most happy sitting in his office writing a book about his slave island, and everyone was cool with that. James was a huge Bettie Page fan, so for his birthday one year, I found an artist at one of the cons who had some beautiful Bettie Page pictures. I got the Ladies to chip in, and we managed to get him this great picture. He became a friend of the Chateau, and I later learned that he knew Bettie Page. He had been trying to get her to do a radio interview, and she agreed to do it from the Chateau. I was so excited she was coming and even more so when the artist arranged for me to meet her. She was meeting a lawyer that day as well and needed a witness to her will, and she asked yours truly to be that witness. I felt so honored.

She was lovely and still looked the same, really, just a little older. She had the same haircut as when she was younger, and she was so down to earth. She wore a red flannel shirt and blue jeans

that day, which suited her adorable Kentucky drawl. I was such a geek that I asked for her autograph, and she signed a little trading card of herself for me, which I later gifted to my eldest son, who is a huge Bettie Page fan. She never understood all the hoopla over her but that made her even more interesting in my eyes. What a treat that was for me!

As in any job, there were Ladies from all walks of life. Some were lost souls, and there were also very confident and bright young women working there. One of these was Nita. Nita was a beautiful submissive of Thai descent with long black hair down her back. She was very seductive and a wonderful submissive. She knew how beautiful she was and reveled in it. She loved walking around the dungeon naked, which was a bit annoying to some for obvious reasons. For some reason, she took to me, and we grew very close. She was 19 years old, and I admired her so much. She was everything I wished I could have been as a submissive. She was perfect. We developed a mother-daughter relationship over time, and she loved serving me. I was very appreciative and grateful that she chose me. It was everything to me.

As time went on, with the help of Mistress Stormy, I became more confident with my skills as a Dominant. I was naturally submissive, so transitioning into a Dominant position was bittersweet for me. Unfortunately, as in life, age is not kind to women or submissives as they age. I started when I was thirty, so I

was already at a disadvantage. I was one hell of a submissive, though, and I was enormously proud of my reputation as a submissive. I was legendary if I may not so humbly say. I was a bit of a Diva, but I knew I was a badass sub, so why not? Becoming a Dominant was not something I really wanted to do, but I had bills to pay, so I adjusted.

I enjoyed most of my time at the Chateau. It is always about the Ladies and the sisterhood that is formed in a club. There is, of course, a competitive edge to things, but you can believe we would have each other's backs in an emergency or a crisis. We worked with each other to hone our skills, which made the time go by faster on a slow day, and it was so important to our development as professional players. We were always trying to figure out ways to bring more people into the dungeon.

One year, I came up with the idea to have a theater of sorts. We had no idea if there would be interest or not, but it turned out to be an instant hit. The shows were lots of work, but I enjoyed it very much. They were usually themed, and we used music for every set. The Ladies who participated were great. It broke up the monotony of just doing sessions every day and gave us all a moment to shine. Some of my favorite moments were flogging Nita to "The Emperor's Waltz," complete with a hoop skirt and Marie Antoinette wig. "Frankie Goes to Hollywood" was the music for doing six different forms of bondage at the time of the song. The holidays were great fun dressing the Ladies up like reindeer and prancing

them all in.

We always had meetings and discussed everything that was going to happen during the show. As we all know, shit happens, and sometimes in a big way. Two Ladies were going to do a sword dance during the show and oddly showed up in Gestapo uniforms. I was behind the stage and had no idea what was going on until one of the Ladies came running into my room shaken and telling me they were interrogating this poor sub on stage.

While this all was being relayed to me, all of a sudden, the stage door that went into my room was quickly opened, a sub was thrown to the ground, and the door was slammed. I ran out of the room to see what the hell was going on and stopped the scene. They had thrown the sub into a faux "gas chamber" after the interrogation. I was mortified, but I had to deal with the task at hand, which was changing the subject. I was running around like a maniac; we had to get the reindeer out, and I had to get James to come and apologize to the audience.

The absurdity of the chaos is still fresh in my mind, along with the sense of panic. I had no time to deal with the faux "Nazis" at that moment. That would be James' job. James was pissed, and he did apologize, and then the eight reindeer came hoofing in, and they were so adorable and unorganized, it was a hit. Needless to say, I was so upset and spent the rest of the night apologizing to the guests, who were very understanding and forgiving. James handled the

Ladies, and they were not asked to perform ever again.

Sometimes, ideas were good, and sometimes they were downright nuts! YMCA (Young Men's Correctional Academy) was my favorite show. The best part of this show was that all of us were dressed like the Village People. We tried to make the shows relatable to everyone. We did the "Story of Jo," and our last was "Bound in Glory," which we filmed. It was a great creative outlet, and it made me proud. At the end of every show, there would be a man sitting in the audience dressed in a suit and tie with flowers in his hands. This was Bill, my one-and-only male slave who was totally devoted to me and adored me. He was a good slave. He was not demanding, which may sound weird to say but a lot of slaves are. I loved being adored, and no other slave was better at it than Bill. I still care for him to this day.

Another beautiful Lady named Janet came into my life at the Chateau. She was a masochist and had a puppy-dog look that was hard to ignore when she wanted something. She was a worker. She worked her ass off for me and loved it. The fact that she was a masochist made her perfect for me. We were playing in the lobby one day for shits and giggles, and there was a whipping post there which I had attached her to. I was using a very heavy whip on her, and I was not too big on warm-ups.

She was poetry in motion as the flogger hit her. She was strong, and the way she would channel the pain was to pull herself up the

whipping post every time I struck her. It was art, and it was moving, so she gave that to me. I always have an appreciation for submissives who have no agenda and just love to serve or go that extra mile because that is the kind of submissive I was. I understand where it comes from and what a satisfying feeling it was to give that gift to someone. She made me feel incredibly special.

One day, I came to work, and James added a new piece of art to his wall. It was the picture of Marilyn Monroe that my father had made me look at when he first molested me. It really triggered me, and I was not sure what I was going to do or how I was going to handle looking at it every day. I finally got up the nerve to go to his office and ask him to take it down or move it to a less conspicuous spot and explain to him the reason for the request. He was unmoved and, like a lot of people throughout my life, suggested I just move on and get over it. He was not moving the picture. I lost so much respect for the man in that one moment. I continued to work there but saw him in a different light and just stayed away from him from that point forward. Shame on him.

# SCOTTISH BOB

One day, I was sitting back in my dungeon, which I call "my" dungeon, because James gave it to me to decorate and use as my

own in appreciation for all my help and work I did at the Chateau. Nita came running into my room and said, "Mistress, you have to come with me!" She was very excited and a little beside herself. I followed her to another room, and standing in that room was my Scottish Bob. We had lost each other when I moved to The Chateau. I was very fond of him and sad that I had "lost" him. He came into the session with Nita. I had since changed my name to Mistress Hillary, so he was not able to find me.

It was beautiful when we saw each other, and I gave him the biggest hug I could. He always wore soft sweaters, which all the Ladies liked fondling, including myself. I had seen Scottish Bob at The Dominion. I was his first session ever. Back then, we recommended a first-timer switch in session if they were not sure of their status. We were in the room maybe five minutes before he decided he was not submissive, and we would switch roles. It was so nice. He was a Dominant for sure but did not want to hurt me. I had to teach him that it was okay and that he was not hurting me. I liked it, and I needed it. It took some time. My favorite was when I tried to get him to use a cane on me, and he was certain he could not ever use such a brutal instrument. Later, it became his toy of choice.

After talking for a while, we decided that we should do a double session with Nita. He would have to be submissive, though, because I was a big bad Domme now. We went back to my room. The bondage table in the room was big enough for two people. I was a

little nervous about this, I have to say. I tied them both up side by side on the table to the sounds of Bolero. Never was there ever a bigger flop of a session than me trying to top Scottish Bob. I was using all my best moves, and he was not buying it for a second. It was comical, actually, and I was humiliated and humbled. Once the session was over, we finally talked after Nita left the room. We laughed about the absurdity of the session, and I told him if he came back, I would be submissive to him, which was the natural order of things for the two of us.

Scottish Bob returned to see me alone, and everything was right. As a rule, I tended to be attracted to more aggressive, arrogant men, which obviously never worked for me. He was a kind and gentle man and open to feedback when we played because he wanted to learn to do things the right way. I always appreciated the equal playing field, so to speak. I always felt unique and important in a room with him.

We were able to revisit our proper roles before he had to leave for England, and the session was terrific. I was on a happy high when we were finished, but I felt a pain in my gut that he would be leaving, and I did not know when I would see him again. We said our goodbyes, and I cried, knowing how much I would miss him and the magic he brought to my life. About two hours later, he walked in the door again. I was flabbergasted. He had been thinking about our session and felt he did not give me a big enough tip, so he drove from Orange County to bring me more. Talk about feeling special!

Yes, I would miss this man and think of him often.

He invited me to go away with him to a resort for the weekend. As fate would have it, I had just married M. I stupidly just told him I had nothing to wear to a fancy resort, and I could not go. I was in love with M but felt drawn to Bob as a guiding light and felt so deliciously subby when I was with him. His accent was so sexy, and I hung on his every word. While he did not have the mechanics of the equipment down, his ego did not get in the way of wanting to learn things either. So many Doms who passed through the doors of the clubs I worked at just had the attitude that they were Dominant and could do no wrong. I was bought and paid for, and whatever the damage was done was okay because that was what they paid for. Just as in sex, it is nice to consider the likes and dislikes of the submissive. It makes for better play and a more appreciative and devoted sub.

# REUNITED

I cannot recall the exact date, but I think it was in the autumn of 1995. I was working and was called to the reception area to take a phone call. This was not something we were allowed except under special circumstances. The receptionist was a sweet Lady and made

sure I got the call. I picked up the phone, and it was Mistress Suzette from Lady Laura's. I had worked with Mistress Suzette for years prior to leaving Lady Laura's, and she was a pretty straight shooter. She told me that she felt I should know, even though everyone had been sworn to secrecy, and I was not going to find out that Lady Laura was very ill. My heart hurt when she told me. She could not talk long but said she felt I was entitled to know because of my close relationship with Lady Laura. I was so grateful to her for this call, and I thanked her.

I did not know how I was going to handle this because my first instinct was to get in my car and see Laura. I thought about it for some time and decided to give Laura the choice of whether she wanted to see me or not in a particular way. I sent her a dozen long-stemmed pink roses with a note that said I was here if you wanted me, along with my phone number. The next day, she phoned me. She told me as soon as she got the roses, she knew who they were from before she opened the card. I decided to visit her the next day.

I was so nervous and still unsure about how she would feel about me after all this time. It had been three years since we had last spoken, and I had gone to work for her nemesis. I drove to her house and walked with fear and anticipation to the front door. As soon as we saw each other, I felt a wave of emotions go through me. We immediately hugged each other, and things felt like we had never parted. I had come back home. She was still beautiful, but I could

see in her eyes a sadness I had never known in her. We sat and talked for hours. Things were not good. She had been diagnosed with multiple myeloma, but she was optimistic. She had stopped smoking a year prior to contracting it, and she was proud of that. She was getting ready to move out of her home, which surprised me. David was no longer in her life. He had fucked her over, as we all knew he would, and it was a heartbreaking story. Why do we trust so much when we love? Why do we lose ourselves in our blessed bliss of feeling loved and give ourselves up to these wretched predatory men? It just felt so wrong to see this happen to Lady Laura. She was our hero and our guiding light. She was a badass woman who, in the end, just wanted to be loved.

While David was in her life, even before I left, she let him into her business and eventually into her bank account. He started "paying the bills" and managing the money. Lady Laura did very well for herself. She had a lovely home in the Beverly-Fairfax area of Los Angeles, which she was proud of. I learned during our conversation that he had not been paying the bills and mismanaging her money to his benefit. Her house was in foreclosure, and she had to move into her mother's home in Fullerton now. This was so heartbreaking to see and so humiliating for Lady Laura. He had gone back to Kansas City because there was nothing left of her by the time he was finished.

I offered myself to her and insisted I was here to help and take care of her. She was my chosen Mother, and though we had a spat,

all was forgiven as it now seemed so petty and unimportant. She was still running the business but more in spirit. I tend to dive into situations and want to fix everything no matter what it takes, and this was one of those times.

What did she need from me? This time together was so bittersweet. We laughed and talked about the good old days, and we also tried to come up with our battle plan to make her better. She was optimistic, and I was going to fix everything. Everything was going to be okay, right? I had to be there for her. Nothing in life would keep me from that. Lady Laura became my life again, and I was honored that she loved me that much!

So, how was I going to manage this? I was still working for James, and I felt I should continue that because he gave me a job when I needed one. The next day, I had to go to work. I went into his office to tell him that I would be helping Laura, but I had every intention of staying with him and working. He was skeptical. I always found situations like this strange to me because I have always been a woman of my word and very loyal to people who have been good to me. It always saddened me that people could not trust that about me because I cannot understand anyone being anything other than loyal and operating with integrity under these circumstances. He agreed we would give it a try, and I thanked him.

Laura moved into her Fullerton home, and the lovely little house we all loved so much in Edinburgh was now gone and up for

sale. I was still married, and, honestly, I just told M how things were going to go. I lived in North Hollywood, so I could easily go to work, but after work, I would go to Fullerton to see Laura, and then I would go back home at night. Laura did have children who were living in her mother's house, but eventually they found other housing. Some of the kids (like her youngest son, who was the apple of her eye) were very helpful, as you would expect one's children to be when going through something like this. However, some were not. They were born-again Christians who always reviled her for what she did for a living but had no problem taking money from her "ill-gotten gains." I remember them driving from Orange County to "borrow" money from her, and she would go out to the car and give it to them. As parents, we want our children to love us, and we want to make their lives better. It would have been nice if some love had been given in return. They were very hypocritical and not very nice.

The more time I spent with Laura, the less James liked it, and he began harassing me and bad-mouthing me. I could feel things were not going well with him, but I knew it was not because of me. I did everything I promised. I continued to help with Chateau events. That year, there were a lot of events because it was a big anniversary year (maybe 25), so there was a big soiree planned once a month to celebrate the anniversary.

One of the events was a slave hunt, which none of the staff was keen on. The way he wanted this to work was to have clues to where submissives were hiding outside of the Chateau, such as the local

grocery store, and then the clients could go and find them and pick them up. Not a great scene for any sub with a stranger, I would think, but this was his one big idea for the year, and he was adamant it was going to happen. The Ladies had expressed their unwillingness to do this, and, of course, it was my influence that swayed them in this direction in his mind. In the meantime, I got a call from my brother that my biological mother was ill, and I needed to go to Michigan to see her.

I told James I had to go, and he kind of mumbled me away like a grumpy old man. I told him I would be back. But during my visit, James decided to fire me. The Ladies had kept in contact with me during all of this, and it seems he had come up with a compromise for the Ladies, something to the effect of "go somewhere and hide your panties, and the clients can search for those and come back and see the sub whose panties he had found." Since no one was keen on getting caught hiding their panties in the produce section of the grocery store, that was evidently my fault. He did not like the influence I had over the Ladies, and frankly, I could not have been less interested in a situation than I was in this one.

I came back home and had no job. This made me angry. I went in to talk to James and made him see the error of his ways somehow, and he invited me back. I was bitter about it and vowed I would only be there long enough to tell my clients I was leaving, and they could find me back at Lady Laura's. Peace out to ya, James.

Eventually, I started taking Laura to her doctor's appointments, stopping in at the business for her to pick up whatever money had been taken in, and checking in on the Ladies. Laura's illness and her distance from the business made it very difficult for her to be on-site. I could see that things were not right, but I needed to prioritize what was important, and that was Lady Laura. Once I left the Chateau, I was in the business, and I heard some unscrupulous business practices were being practiced by some of the ladies. Later, I learned that Lady Laura knew of it, but she did not have the energy to deal with it, and all that mattered was her life at that time. It hurt her deeply. I could not speak to it because I was an outsider to most of those who were there for such a long time. I was quiet and just did what I needed to do to help Laura. I was spending more and more time with her at her home, and as time went on, there were more doctors' appointments.

Things seemed hopeless, but then she got into the City of Hope, which gave Laura real hope that she would be okay. I went with her to see the doctors, and she was hoping to get a stem-cell transplant. She went through the agony of the bone marrow test and all the other tests that went with it, only to be told that she would not be able to have the surgery because her lungs were so damaged from all the smoking she had done in the past. She would not have the capacity to survive the surgery because of this. This was a real gut punch for her. She had been so proud of the fact that she had quit smoking a year prior to contracting the disease that this was heartbreaking to

hear.

This was her last hope.

Before she received her diagnosis, she had been seeing a doctor who happened to be a client who decided her troubles were all in her back. He fused her spine, which changed the way she looked and walked. She later learned, of course, this was all incorrect and never forgave the doctor for his bullshit diagnosis.

So now what? The slap of reality had hit us both. There was no cure for My Lady, and we both cried many tears together over this. Eventually, one must snap out of it and become strong, which we both did. Laura was still pretty strong at this time, so she carried on and began to get her affairs in order. I was amazed at her strength. The day we went to Forest Lawn together, she put together her own funeral and picked out her headstone, and I was in awe of her.

Overall, she went about her life as business as usual. She spent time with her family. As in a lot of families, there was tension with some of the children. Oh, the misdeeds of a mother that are punishable for life! Children don't seem to be able to forgive sometimes. I tried to stay out of the family matters, but eventually, I landed smack dab in the middle of it all.

One day, when I was with Laura at her home, she told me she wanted to talk to me. I sat down with her and could tell this was a serious conversation, but I did not know what to expect. Lady Laura

began to speak to me about our relationship and how much like her own daughter I had always been to her. We had loved each other from the day we met. We had spoken in the past before David about her making me a partner in the business one day. I had spent so much of my life at Lady Laura's, and when I wasn't doing sessions, I was sitting at the desk answering phones or cleaning the building early in the morning before opening. Before the big fight, I was pretty much running the business for her. She had spent a lot of time with David and sort of lost interest in being at work. She was loving life until it kicked her in the ass.

Laura wanted to leave the business to me. I don't know how many different emotions came over me when she told me. I was flabbergasted, frightened, and honored all at the same time. I did not know what to say. I was concerned about her family and how they would feel. She was concerned her family would shut the business down, and she did not want that. She told me that she knew I would carry on her legacy. It was so important to Laura that her Dominion carry on. I needed to think about it before I made this promise to her. It took me a couple of days of reflection before I decided I could do it. I would never have been the Grand Diva, which was Lady Laura. I would never be able to fill her boots, and I knew that. I always saw myself as a worker bee, and what's more, I was a submissive. How would that work? I realized that my submissive side was my strength and how I had dealt with most things throughout my life, and doing this for my Mistress would be an honor I would humbly accept. I

would be able to promise to keep her legacy alive.

Laura eventually told the staff, and it went over like a lead balloon! This would become one of the most terrifying times of my life. When I went to work either to session or to stop by and check on things before seeing Laura, I was harassed, yelled at, physically assaulted, and called an opportunist by staff members. I was cornered in the back room and screamed at and threatened on a couple of occasions, and someone keyed the word PIG across the side of my car. I never told Laura these things. I didn't keep very calm, but I did carry on.

All our time together became so sweet and beautiful. We cherished every second and really did not talk about the inevitable unless we had to. I had already started paying the bills and taking care of her finances. Laura wanted to make the transition as smooth as possible for me, so she took me to banks and lawyers to make sure things would be settled. Her family was livid. I have to say it was shocking how unkind some of her kids could be to her. Now that I am older and have experienced it myself, it is a heartbreaking feeling. Laura did not back down.

As the disease started to take over, she began getting weaker physically. She wanted a Christmas party with her girls, and we made that happen. Laura always made sure everyone had a place to go on Thanksgiving every year and was famous for her mac-and-cheese. We used to have Christmas parties that were more like

"Let's get drunk on Grasshoppers and give each other presents." They were always eventful, and there was always a delightful story to tell after a Christmas party. It was not hard to ask the ladies to come to the party even though the distance was a bit far. Several of them had been out to visit Laura before, and everyone was on board and happy to be able to see her and spend time with her again at Christmas. It was a beautiful night.

All of us were there with our Lady, sharing memories, being goofy, and sharing the love we all had for Laura. Her tree was trimmed in her favorite colors, black and gold, and I had made enough cookies for an army and had buckets of them stacked to form a tree next to Laura's. I know there were gifts, but I don't remember any of them because it did not matter. We all felt this would be our last time together, and we reveled in it. Laura was so happy to have all her girls around her, and it was just a joy to see her smiling and enjoying the night. Sometimes, you could see her pain, but she hid it well most of the time. This night is one of my fondest memories of all of us together, putting any differences we had aside and taking in all of Lady Laura that we could that night. What a blessing that was!

# IN HER HONOR

I had decided that I wanted to do something special at Lady Laura's to surprise Laura. I decided to redecorate one of the rooms upstairs in a theme that fit Laura's taste and style. It struck me on one of my sleepless nights… Cats! Anyone that knew Lady Laura knew of her love of felines. She drove a Cougar, loved Siegfried and Roy in Las Vegas, and had even met them and their White Lions. She always had cats, and she adored them. There was my theme. Now, to make it sexy!

The walls in what was then called The Green Room were stark white with green Tudor lines resembling the outside of the building with a hideous hunter-green carpet. I searched high and low for a tiger stripe carpet with the walls, and the banister on the spiral staircase painted gold and the trim in the room black. The bondage table was recovered in a leopard print. The finishing touch was a throne with lions' heads and arms. It took me months to get this finished. I was so excited.

I changed the name of the room to Lady Laura's Lair. I could not wait for her to see it. The disease was wreaking havoc on my Lady, and every day, you could see her losing a little bit of ground but never losing hope. One day, I finally got her over to the dungeon, and I was so excited for her to see her room. The thought never had occurred to me that she would be unable to make it up the stairs to

see it. She gave it a try, but it was just not going to happen. I felt so bad and a little selfish that I had never considered this. It was a sad moment for both of us, but she hugged me, told me she loved me, and said she could not wait to see the pictures. She never got to see her room.

# THE ANGEL

![photo]

*Lady Laura*

As time passed, I was more at work and home less and less. I started staying with Laura most days, and her kids stayed at night. Laura did go through chemotherapy, but it did not touch the disease. We spent more and more time at the doctors' offices. It is a strange thing to try to describe because even though everything was so tragic and sad, every moment was so sweet and beautiful.

Lady Laura was my chosen Mother, my friend, mentor, and Mistress. I was her chosen daughter, and we adored each other. I felt so honored that she allowed me to take care of her and be there with her for her journey. At the end of October 1997, things got to be too much for her. She had been determined she was going to stay home, but she needed to go to the hospital. I don't remember exactly how long she was there exactly. I was with her every day. I slept in her room every night. We spent hours talking, and I usually slipped out to give them their time with her when she had a visitor.

Then, one day, she slipped into a coma. My heart was broken, as we weren't finished. It could not be time yet. I was screaming inside, "Don't leave me – it is too soon!" Again, my selfishness. Laura was in pain; she had been on morphine for some time, and she was less and less awake. I stayed with her as much as I could. I still had a family, and I had to let the Ladies know what was going on, so I would leave for a time, but I returned to be with her every night.

On November 5, 1997, I was sitting in the room with her, and suddenly, she just bolted up out of her sleep and started talking to

me. It was amazing. We talked for four hours about everything. Every word she spoke to me was a gift. Then, suddenly, in the middle of our conversation, her nose began to bleed, and she looked at me. I swear she looked like an angel. She was glowing. She could no longer speak, but she spoke to me with her eyes. I have never seen an expression on anyone's face like the one on Lady Laura's. She truly became an angel in front of my eyes.

She was saying goodbye to me, and I knew it. A barrage of nurses and doctors invaded the room, and she was lying there on the bed. I held her hand. Some family had managed to get there in time to say goodbye, but I never left her. Then, a moment came when I felt a wind-like rush go through my heart, and her spirit entered me like a great wind and left me just as quickly. Lady Laura left this Earth on November 5, 1997. This was one of my life's saddest yet most intense and beautiful moments, and I shall never forget it; it still haunts me to this day. I can still see her angelic face and that smile in her eyes.

As time passed, I would feel her guiding me, and I would subconsciously find myself doing things the way she used to do them, and I knew she was with me. Lady Laura was my blessing.

Her service was held several days later. My first experience of being involved in a will-reading was sad and disappointing. The family was fighting over pieces of jewelry, and everyone was pissed off by the end of the reading. I was so uncomfortable because I knew

they weren't fond of me, and Lady Laura had left me pieces of her jewelry that were significant to her, which I did share with some of the Ladies of the Dominion.

I was just so sad, and everything was so ugly up to and including her funeral service. I had ordered my Lady a blanket of sterling roses for her casket. She was dressed in her shiniest outfit, and I had put a bottle of White Diamonds perfume in because she would have liked that. The service was held in a small chapel at the cemetery, and on one side sat the family; on the other, her Dominion family and friends from years gone by came to pay respects.

Judging from the program, Laura did not have a hand in her service. Laura had returned to church long before her illness, so it was a Christian service. We all expected her family to speak; none of us on the sinners' side of the chapel had been asked. Her son-in-law, whom she despised and who was an absolute hypocrite, got up and gave a speech and started it by saying that *Laura was going to hell!* I became frozen with anger, not able to say anything. It was an awful thing to do, but so typically "born again" of him to become her judge and jury. I had always been under the impression that it was more up God's alley.

Thank God that one woman in the room was a true badass and had the guts to stand up to this vile person and speak up for Lady Laura. Lady Olivia Outré – never one who was afraid to speak her mind – just stood up and gave him hell! She talked about all the good

that Lady Laura had done in the world and how kind, generous, and loving she was. She was not having it, and I loved her for it. I was so proud of her; as far as I was concerned, she was the Queen of Badassery after that!

# TRANSITION

I don't know how long we were closed. Time was a blur to me then, and I was on autopilot getting through my days. I cried and cried until there were no tears left to cry, and then I found some more. I had to get back to work because so many people relied on Lady Laura to pay the bills. I opened her back up, and I put myself in the mindset that I was going to be strong and make Laura proud.

A transition like this is never easy, and I was naïve and already beaten up mentally by those who had already made their opinions known about me before my Lady passed. Some Ladies were supportive of me, and there were some who would have been just as happy if I had never come in to work at all.

Many people felt I had returned to Laura to "take over" the dungeon. This was never even a thought in my mind. My only thought was that I loved her and needed to be with her and take care of her. People thought I was manipulative, coercive, or just downright evil for receiving what was considered the blessing of Lady Laura's Dominion. I don't think people really realized everything that was going on behind the scenes and the chaos the dungeon was in. Lady Laura was drowning in debt, and were it not for the generosity of Sir Robert, we would have surely been shut down due to a lousy loan shortly after Laura's passing.

A lot was going on at the dungeon that I had been watching

while I was caring for Laura, and I just took a mental inventory. Other things were more important, such as how Laura did not need to know how bad things had gotten there while she was sick. I found it shameful and disgusting and now I had to fix it. There was no "take it slow" mode for me. Drugs were circulating at the dungeon and all the expected behaviors that went with it. There was a bit of a free-for-all attitude and a lot of things going on that shouldn't have been. Ladies were doing sessions they had no business doing that were dangerous.

The most disappointing and sad thing for me was the Ladies were doing sessions off the books while Laura was sick. Lady Laura knew this, and it broke her heart. A reliable source told me it had been happening before I came back, so these women had been stealing from Laura for a long time. There were a few Ladies who professed love for Lady Laura but somehow felt they could justify their behavior because "the drugs made them do it." They also felt that doing sessions after hours meant they did not have to give Laura her due.

But back in those days, there were no after-hours. Those were the days we stayed if people were coming to the door, and we would sometimes play until 3 or 4 in the morning. I found this all to be so despicable and sad. It was shocking to me. I had to make many decisions and changes, which would not be easy, but getting rid of liars and backstabbers was not a second thought for me. The Lady

had been there for them and had helped them for years, and they were going to steal from her while she was dying? I have no place in my life for people like this. To me, it is unforgivable.

My nature is to do things right because I believe that I will be able to sleep more easily at night. I just have too much anxiety to do things any other way. I knew the wolves would be out for blood now that Lady Laura had passed, and I was right. I received threats from competitors regarding zoning issues, tax issues, and threats to get us closed down. Lady Laura was also drowning in debt and in danger of having to close in a matter of months. Money had been mismanaged, and there was also the matter of a $60,000 balloon payment due on a loan Laura took out for the business.

All the people that were so angry at me when Laura decided to leave me her legacy would never have been able to keep the business going. It was so shaky, and no one knew it. I had to make changes that the Ladies did not like to protect us. I had to clean the place up. I instituted a no-drugs policy. BDSM and drugs don't mix, period. It is dangerous to play under the influence, whether you're a top or a bottom. There were things going on that would be questionable to law enforcement should they come in, such as a drawer full of vibrators, dildos, and condoms. Penetration of any kind was considered a sex act, and honestly, I just felt it was so unhygienic that I was happy to take the drawer and dump it into the dumpster.

I wanted to change the thought process for play. The Ladies

were livid and did not know how they would do their sessions without the vibrators. It was so easy to "torture" someone with a vibrator, and it usually made the sessions very short for some. During all the upset over this move, when the Ladies would ask me why, I would explain all the obvious reasons to them and add the one I felt was the most important. BDSM starts in the mind; if you can get into someone's mind, the session will be much better. In all honesty, the clients were not upset about these missing items. As time went on, I was proven correct. Sessions became longer, and the clients were happier. Some of the Ladies surprised themselves at how good they were in session when they had to push themselves a little. I was proud of myself for setting the new boundaries and of the Ladies for adapting.

Being one of the Ladies myself, I wanted more respect from the clients. This whole mentality that sex workers are victims or desperate or can be bought and sold had to end.     I wanted the Ladies treated as such. The Ladies, who were professional players, represented all walks of life. I let them know I would not be referring to them as girls any longer. They would be addressed as the Ladies that they were.

They deserved respect, and again, this would be a teachable moment for both the clients and the Ladies. I had worked for over 15 years by now, and I always abhorred the disrespect we were given and the exploitation some of us suffered under our boss's eye. I told

the staff I would never ask them to break a rule for any reason. It became a joke of sorts when I told them if a client is asking for sexual favors, just tell them that they must ask me, and if I said yes, it is a go. I was surprised how many clients thought they were the special ones who were above the rules.

We did not have a nudity license, and I think the rule that upset the clients more than anything was the Ladies had to keep the G-string on. I don't know too many Ladies who were upset by this rule, which made life so much simpler for the subs, especially. Some of them started wearing a G-string, a thong, and a pair of panties, which I thought was great!

I think a lot of people expected me to drive the business into the ground and fail. I never gave it a second thought. I just did what I thought was best, and I think working from the perspective of my sub side was always a bonus for me. I was very empathetic to the Ladies' problems, and since the place was clean, I made sure they all knew I would have no problem calling the police if we had any issues. That is just one of the good things about having your house in order.

We did have visits from the city and Building and Safety, all brought on by complaints from competitors, not the public. We had Vice come in, and everything was okay. The police were very good to us and never bothered us. There was actually a time when the police would stop in for coffee, which was really cool but not good

for business while they were there, so eventually, I had to explain to them it was bad for business for them to be sitting in the lounge! The good thing was they knew we were on the up-and-up and everything was in order.

I had to go to Vice once to advise on someone they were looking for. I was nervous, but they were so kind to me and very complimentary of our place because they knew it was clean and that we followed the law. I was proud of myself. We were cool with the police, but the fire departments loved us! It was an ongoing joke sometimes how many inspections we would get in a week or, better yet, in a day at times. The Ladies were pleased to show them where all the fire extinguishers were. I later learned I was being taken when Francesca told me that only our local fire department should have been coming to do the inspections. We had them coming in from all over the city. We never minded, though, as it was kind of funny, and it was great when they came back alone, off-duty, to play.

It also made me happy when Ladies came to me looking for work, and they told me they wanted to work for me because they were sober and wanted to work in a drug-free atmosphere. I did my best to keep it that way. But it was not easy at times. I was very adamant about this policy. I had seen too many lives destroyed by drugs, and I wanted to protect Lady Laura and the Ladies that were there. I hated it when I learned someone was doing drugs. Let's face it: I was not very perceptive in this department. Normally, another

lady would tell me, and I also had so many sober Ladies working for me; they knew all the signs.

I had to make some heartbreaking decisions about letting people go. It wasn't hard when I first had the place because I was not emotionally invested in a lot of the women working at the time, simply because of the deceit and what I considered an abuse of Lady Laura's trust and kindness. So that was easy. It was the BDSM babies that I raised who had fallen from grace. Ladies I had trained and raised and had great affection for. It had to be done to keep the staff and the house safe, and this was the big picture I had to look at. I was so proud when I met someone who said, "We know your place is clean." That was an accomplishment.

One day, a client came running into the business in a panic with a bright orange piece of paper in hand. Someone had hired some non-English speaking people to pass flyers out in our neighborhood that said we were running a brothel. Everyone jumped into action, got dressed, and went around the neighborhood, taking them off porches and car windows. Of course, we missed some. One of the Ladies who spoke Spanish caught up with the guys who had no idea what they were passing out, and they said someone gave them forty dollars to pass them out in the neighborhood. The plan backfired for whoever passed them out because we got calls from our neighbors supporting us, which was a wonderful feeling.

There was one incident that I still laugh about to this day

because it reminded me of the Keystone Cops. I was usually stuck inside most of the day, but I wanted to go out and get some fresh air on one particular day, so I walked up the corner to get a soda. I wasn't gone for 10 minutes, and I was on my way back, and I could see a scatter of Ladies coming out of the business from the back through the parking lot. They were still in their gear! WTF! There was an iron-furniture store on the corner, and one of the Ladies dressed in her assless chaps had run in there.

My phone rang, and she told me she was hiding in the store to call me, and they did not know she was there. She freaked out because "The City" had entered the building. I got to the business, and standing in the lobby was the man I knew from Building and Safety, who was looking very confused at the scene that ensued when he walked in the door. He had just come by to talk to assure me our business license was okay, and everyone just scrambled. I apologized, and, like myself, he thought it was funny. Oh, you Ladies of little faith and trust in me.

One of the toughest times was when James was trying to get us closed AGAIN, and he reported us to Building and Safety, saying we were not properly zoned. This was not the case, as we were in a commercial/residential building, which was one of the reasons Lady Laura bought it. This did open a large can of worms and we started getting hassled by the city.

By then, Scottish Bob had become a very important part of my

life, and his title had become Sir Robert. I have terrible anxiety, so I hated dealing with things like this, but Robert was very good at it, so he started helping me deal with legal problems, lawyers, et cetera. This turned into a very tense and emotional nightmare. I was unsure if I could keep the dungeon open with the city in my house.

We had to go down to the LA City Council and meet our representative, who was genuinely nice to us. He told us what was going on and that there would be a hearing we would have to attend to determine whether we could stay open. It was weeks before this would happen. We had to seek legal representation, and we found the best lawyer in town who had dealt with many adult businesses and succeeded. We had to come up with a huge retainer, and he charged $650 an hour. I was astonished but up against a wall. I do have to say, in retrospect, he was worth every penny, though it was rough at the time.

While we were waiting for the hearing, we learned that City Council members had been going door-to-door in the neighborhood talking to neighbors to get their feedback on us, and no one had anything bad to say about us. They were glad we were there because it made them feel safer, and we were respectful of them. Some just thought every neighborhood needed "a little color," as they put it, and we were their "color in the neighborhood" story. This was a good thing.

The great thing was when Robert went down to City Hall a few

days before the hearing to look at the files on the case, which he found unheard of that there were testimonials from neighbors, a realtor, and, of all things, a local pastor encouraging the council to let us stay. $75,000 and a million frazzled nerves later, we got a call the day before we were supposed to go to the hearing, and they had called it off! My guardian angel had my back again!

This was all further proof to me that doing things the right way was the best way for me.

# GROWING PAINS

I spent most of my time running the business. It was all-encompassing. I am a bit of a control freak and did everything myself at first. It was my reputation on the line now. I knew things were clean the way I wanted them and stayed on top of it throughout the day. There was still a lot of anger and resentment from some of the staff, and this was a very uncomfortable situation at times. I understood, and I put up with it for a long time. I struggled at times because a lot of the Ladies who had been in the scene longer than I tended to question my judgment. They treated me like I was a stupid submissive and incapable of making good decisions. A lot of them mentored me, and I respected them, but they did not seem to respect me as the new owner. They could not get past the "Bunny" side of me. Who would have thought that a submissive woman could have a brain and be capable of running a business? As the years passed, I realized *ONLY* a submissive woman would have had the strength to put up with what I did to make the business work. I tried to keep everyone happy, but that was just not possible. I was trying to make positive changes, but I had to do it slowly. Not all the Ladies were on board with some of the changes.

Over time, hiring new staff and training them in my way of doing things was helpful to the transition. I wanted everyone who came to work for me to be informed and know exactly what was

expected of them. I wanted them to know that they never had to do anything they were not comfortable with. This was hugely important to me because, in the past, there had been pressure to do sessions you did not want to do, and it was very uncomfortable. There were great nonfiction books to learn from, which I made required reading for neophytes when they began working with me. '*Screw The Roses and Send Me the Thorns*' by Phillip Miller and '*Molly Devon and SM 101*' by Jay Wiseman. These were all a great source of information and advice and pretty much covered most of what one needed to know to play safely.

The responsibility I felt for the safety of new Ladies was real, and I am sure I was deemed overprotective by many. There were serious protocols in place for new subs. Once hired, they needed to be trained, and that started with being shadowed on the first day or two to ensure they learned how to conduct an interview properly. The interview was the contract for the session, and limits had to be set, along with safe words. Normally, a senior staff member would sit in on the interview and help pick out the equipment for the session. If you were brand new to the scene, you were not allowed to use rope. Only leather cuffs, leather paddles, and a light flogger were allowed. No gags or blindfolds or any of the heavy equipment like canes or wood paddles were permitted. We always explained to the Ladies that there would be a pretty good chance you would get bruised your first few days until you learned how to control your session. Arnica was a staple, and so were ice packs in the freezer for

sore bottoms!

It was very important to me that everyone was trained. It was confusing for them at times, though, because some of the senior staff would change the rules to what they thought was best.

Eventually, I had to rely on others to help me with reception because working seven days a week was too much for anyone. The people I chose to do this were Ladies I had grown up with and trusted. They were my mentors and had taught me a lot, and they were also close to Lady Laura. While I am totally of the Old School, and I pretty much stuck to those values when bringing in new Ladies, sometimes one must make compromises. The biggest disagreements were so petty sometimes, and one major one was submissives wearing black. I was a firm believer in submissives wearing pastel colors and not black. When I was a submissive, I never wore black, and I loved to dress in frilly, ruffle outfits all the time. I was wearing pigtails in my hair in my mid-30s to dress the part. I always felt that costumes and appropriate clothing were a very important part of BDSM protocol.

When I became the owner and hired people, I formed a different outlook on this subject, much to the disappointment of my mentors. Normally, people in the scene have the gear they put on when they go out, and most of the time it was black, especially when goth came into the picture. I made compromises because a lot of Ladies could not just go out and buy a new wardrobe, and I did not want them to

until they had started making money and were sure they would be staying. This decision went over like a lead balloon. I was certain clients would be able to tell the difference between a Domme and a sub because I did require the subs to wear a collar and no thigh-high boots. Things were fine, and the Ladies did a good job keeping their submissive personalities obvious in their wardrobes.

When I left the building, the Ladies on the desk decided it was their job to give the subs shit for what they were wearing, and made them very uncomfortable. Eventually, this became a huge bone of contention for the Ladies on the desk who were unable to move forward. This was all part of the lack of acceptance of my capabilities to make decisions by the senior staff. I talked to my desk ladies and asked them to stop hassling the subs. I would deal with the dress code, but they just could not do it because they did not take me seriously. I had to let so many of them go just for the disrespect they showed me and the lack of faith they had in me. It wasn't easy because they were my friends and I cared for them very much. Eventually, they were all gone, and sadly, most of them never spoke to me again.

Trust is not something I am good at. I have had great difficulties trusting people my entire life, but the reasons are justifiable. It was sad and strange to me how many of my relationships changed after I started running Lady Laura's. I guess it began with the dysfunction of the desk staff. There had not been paid desk people before. It was

every woman who had the phone for herself, and the person who had the phone had the power. For some reason, clients wanted to see the Lady on the phone. It did give them an unfair advantage because whoever it was could strike up a conversation on the phone with a client and get them to come in and see her. It was important to me to have desk staff that did not work on the floor.

Years prior to Lady Laura's passing, a friend of mine who knew Laura as well was struggling after the local adult paper she worked at closed. I recommended her to Laura, and she let her come in as a Dominant even though she had no formal training. She was older, and starting as a sub was not really an option for her, so she learned as she went and got herself a nice little clientele. She and I became very close friends. She was my maid of honor at my wedding to M, and we spent every Wednesday together. I considered her my dearest friend at the time, and I trusted her implicitly, so when I decided I needed a manager to help me out, she was my obvious choice. It helped her financially, and it helped me so I could have time away from the dungeon. She did this for years for me. As Robert and I became closer, I began traveling and had no reservations, leaving her in charge while I was away. For the purposes of this story, let's call her "Jenni."

I referred earlier to a man named John, who was the slave of my first Mistress, Deidre. He also had one of the first BDSM clubs in Los Angeles in the '70s called Passive Arts, which was short-lived. He was a steady client of Lady Laura's, and I used to have sessions

with him when I was submissive. Shortly after Laura passed, he came to me and wanted to borrow $25,000. He was doing a Dine LA event and had neglected to pay for his advertising. I did not have that kind of money, and I had to turn him down. Our relationship began to change after this. Eventually, his business went bust, and he was looking for something else to do. We talked one day, and he told me he was interested in opening another BDSM club and wondered if I wanted to partner with him. I am not partnering material. If I cannot make it on my own, I would rather not be doing it. I was very nice to him and tried to give him some suggestions. I also told him that clubs run by men were a thing of the past and he would not succeed.

At that time, finally, women had taken over the BDSM world, and all the clubs were run by women. This was a big deal, and I was thrilled about it. There had been so much exploitation by the male owners of the clubs in the past that it was refreshing not to have those concerns anymore. There also seemed to be more peace between the clubs. I brought this up to him and told him I thought he should pursue something else. At the time, BDSM-themed restaurants were the rage in New York, and I suggested he try something like that. He had been a caterer, so it seemed worth a try to me. We were cordial, and that was the end of that, or so I thought.

Months went by, and weird things began to happen when I was away. My best friend and manager, "Elsa," reported to me that one

night, five of the Ladies had sent a slave out to buy them tequila, which was an absolute no. I was livid, but I was in England. I trusted her implicitly, so I told her to let them all go, which she did. When I came back from my trip, an Olivia painting had disappeared from one of the upstairs rooms, and no one knew anything about it. This was a huge painting that took two people to carry, and it happened to be Lady Laura's favorite Olivia piece. I was devastated. It made no sense, and I could not figure out how it was possible for it to just disappear. "Jenni" played dumb, and to this day, I have never been able to find it. One night, I got a phone call from another desk person to tell me that one of the Ladies was leaving because I was letting people have sex in session. This wasn't the case, of course, so I got in my car and came over, hoping I could talk to her, but she just did not believe otherwise. She told me my "Jenni" had told her this, and she believed her, so she quit. Was "Elsa" trying to sabotage me and my business? And if so, why?

I went out of town for a short trip, and when I came back, "Elsa" came to me and told me she was leaving to explore other options for herself. I knew at that instant what was going on, and I confronted her and asked her if she was going to work for John. She denied it, but I knew that was what was going on. A couple of days after her departure, an ad appeared in the local paper with a new club called Lady Elsa's Passive Arts. John was opening a dungeon, and my best friend was going to work for him! This was such a betrayal that I never recovered from it emotionally. I had lost the best friend I had,

and typical of most people I had loved in life, I got screwed again.

I knew I would be okay because I always am. I truly believe that I have an angel or some other higher power looking after me. They have always been there when I have been in crisis, and I am certain they have looked after me in my younger years for sure. Things were always okay once I got through the agony of betrayal, but it left me very jaded, and I have always had difficulty trusting people. Over the years, I learned to keep people at arm's length because that is what I had to do to protect myself. Don't get me wrong; occasionally, I would slip and just love someone at first sight, but every time, it would end badly for me. I think this is why I became a dog person. You can trust a dog.

# BACK TO LIFE

Time passed as it does, and eventually, I became more secure within myself about what I was doing. I was filled with self-doubt when I first took the reins of the business, but as time passed and I made changes to the way things were being done and to the way the rooms looked, business started picking up. I had a good group of Ladies working with me, and it started to feel like family to me. I loved the Ladies, and I felt they cared for me as well. I was proud that Ladies wanted to work with me because they knew it was a sober environment and I had their backs. I had no tolerance for drugs at work. Over the years, I saw drugs destroy too many people I cared about. When I first started in the scene, drugs were everywhere.

Most liked the new rules because it gave them more control over their sessions and who they saw. There was no pressure on the Ladies or the clients to do a session they did not want to do. They had learned to pass sessions on to someone else they thought would be better suited to the scene without making the client feel bad. It was very important to me that the people coming in to play never felt judged. This was supposed to be the place where you could play out your deepest, darkest fantasy with no judgment. Overall, I feel that this was accomplished.

# RITUALS

One of the many things that attracted me to BDSM was the rituals involved in play. I was drawn to lifestyle players who took things as seriously as I did. Collaring ceremonies always touched

me, and I always got a warm and fuzzy feeling inside when I had the honor to witness one. The first ceremony I ever saw was Mistress Holly collaring her slave Dean. I marveled at the devotion he had to her and the amount of pain he was willing to take to show his devotion. This ceremony was simple but intense. The slave stands with legs spread and arms out so every part of his body is accessible to his Mistress. She used a buggy whip on every part of his body. The swish of the whip as it landed on his outstretched arms was delicious, and his silence was beautiful. I loved seeing the red welts rise on his body with each strike of the whip. When she had covered every available space on him, and he took it in silence, he was allowed to kiss her boots. Then, with his head bent down in reverence to her, she put her collar around his neck. I wanted this for myself one day.

I ended up having two collaring ceremonies of my own during my career when I eventually took slaves of my own. In one, I collared my slave Janet, and in the other, I collared my slave Bill. Since I was submissive myself, I had very high expectations. My perception of a BDSM relationship was give-and-take, and I felt a big responsibility for my subs. I never mixed sex with my subs and made it very clear that would never be a possibility. It could get complicated at times for them to keep emotions in check, and I know that my subs loved me as much as I did them. Sometimes, the most devoted and best of subs are those who are denied. It was always a special thing to me to see the adoration they felt for me, and I always

tried to honor that. I think I was a kind and nurturing Domina, as that is my nature, and I pray I brought some positivity to their lives. I am certain they still care for me as I do them.

My Janet wanted me to brand her, which I had never done before. I made her do all the research, and she taught me how to do it. I practiced on a potato for a long time. On the day of the branding, I had a few trusted people in the room with me, and I branded the inside of her thigh with my initial H for my new name, Mistress Hillary. Every once in a while, we had to touch it up. I also took her to get her labia pierced, which was a big deal. She was all decked out in slave markings and wore them proudly.

Now, here is where things get complicated. Janet eventually professed her carnal love to me, and I had to remind her of the conversation we'd had before we ever embarked on our relationship about how sex wasn't a possibility. As a result, she felt neglected. Janet then fell in lust with another Domme at the dungeon, but the relationship was not Domme/sub. The Lady Janet was seeing was not a huge fan of mine, so messing with my sub was no big deal to her because she had no respect. She and Janet decided to get Janet's clitoris pierced one day with nary a "Hey, Hillary, can we do this?" (If you are into BDSM, you will get just how disrespectful this is – if not, I'm sorry.) I learned three days after the event that this happened, and then I called Janet into a room and shut the door. I asked her if it was true, and she said yes. I then told her to take out

the labia rings I had placed there and told her we were done. She was very upset, as was I, but this is how things work in the real BDSM world. I let her go, but years later, we reconnected, and we still care for each other very much.

Once I ran my own dungeon, I tried very hard to instill proper protocol with the Ladies who worked with me. I was very particular about the way the Ladies were trained. My old-school beliefs were that everyone began as a submissive and learned how to be a good submissive before they could ever become a Switch. This is the way Lady Laura did things, as well as most houses at one time. The belief was that if you experienced what a submissive did, you would be a more compassionate and safer Domina in the end. I know that this became a controversial opinion in later years.

The simple fact is that if you have never been to subspace nor experienced the emotions of a submissive, it is exceedingly difficult to give that to a submissive yourself. I understood not everyone had a submissive side, but learning the protocols and rituals of submission from the "bottom" up made for better Dommes. This was the tried-and-true way of doing things for years, and it worked. Some of the best Dommes in Los Angeles started at The Dominion, and I don't think they ever had regrets about the way they learned things. The old traditions were a very important part of the BDSM experience. I also learned so much from my submission, which was very helpful to me during my years as a Domme. I respect the opinions of those who beg to differ with me on this, but that was the

beauty of owning The Dominion. If you did not want to truly learn your art, it was your choice; you could work somewhere else. I did not compromise my principles on this because it was just that important to me.

Another ritual very near and dear to my heart is becoming a Lady. It is not really a ritual; it is more like being knighted, I think. A lot of up-and-comers don't know the significance of the term Lady. The Old Guard knows that it is an honor bestowed on a woman of a certain age or experience level in BDSM by another Lady. I was fortunate enough to be given my title by my magnificent Lady herself. She bestowed it upon me before she passed, and I always tried to honor the privilege. I was honored to be able to pass the torch to Lady Francesca some years later. It really riles up the Old Timers when a new Domme coming from nowhere just takes the name "Lady." It gives us a reason to talk shit. If you are going to work in a new field, do some research! Have some respect.

We also had some lovely little superstitions that we carried on from day one until we closed. We always had a green money candle on the desk. Usually, it was the desk person who lit the candle, and each person had their own little ceremony for lighting it. We lit incense before we opened it and took it through the building. If there were Ladies in the building, we waved it over them and did a little chant. When there were bad vibes in the building that you could totally feel, we saged the building. The best ritual was Mistress

Kay's Money Bunny dance. Kay was a belly dancer, and she would do this delightful little dance at the door, which included seducing the doorknob and then hopping up and down like a bunny and wiggling her nose. It was the best. We had crystals to protect us, and if that didn't work, we would have a huge spiked pole behind the desk that would work very nicely! It was all part of the rich tapestry that made us the colorful bunch we were.

# LEGENDARY FRIENDS

It goes without saying that without our Dominion friends there would not ever have been a Dominion. I am talking about our clients, some of whom have been with us since the beginning with Lady Laura. They kept us going and became more than just clients but special friends who we cared about. They were our regulars, and we normally knew what they expected when they came in and, as a rule, looked forward to their visits.

One of the sweetest pets who visited us was "Doggy." He was already a client of Lady Laura's when I started in the business, and his fantasy never changed. He was my first Domme session, and I was so intimidated by it that I felt sick, but everyone has to start somewhere, and he was the easiest-going guy there was. I had heard him in session before and witnessed his play with other Dommes but never had to carry it off alone. I felt perfectly inadequate but just did things my silly way and treated him like a dog.

Before I started, I found a newspaper for nose-whacking if he was a bad dog and some Hershey Kisses for good-boy treats, and that was pretty much all I had to work with. I had some of the Ladies come in while he did tricks. He loved barking, and by the end of the session, it was like there was a big old hound dog in the room barking at the moon. He was great! I was probably more like a little girl with her puppy, but he was very happy. He spent time with so

many of us, and you always knew he was in the building if you heard howling. He had been visiting us for years, and we loved him.

I had a collar made for him with his name on it because he was so special to us. I never did that for anyone else. He liked to wind down after his session and talk about old movies. It made me smile when we would be talking in the lobby, and he would tell people he was my first Domme session. He seemed very proud of that. He was the only person I ever bought a personal collar for. He was touched the day I gave it to him. It was a studded collar suitable for a big dog with his name on it. We loved him as he loved us.

One of my favorite sessions was one that Lady Laura did with me. Now, this was amazing. Laura did not do sessions. She did the odd cameo or would play a little in the lobby at times, but I never knew her to session with anyone. I could be wrong, but in all my years with her, I never knew she would do an entire session with anyone. I love firefighters, and we had a client who used to come in who was just that. When I heard what he did for a living, I used to beg him to bring his gear in and play.

Not expecting this to ever happen, he made an appointment with me. It was a surprise, though. Laura had me go up to the room once he got there and wait for him. No problem, subs do this all the time! Well… in comes Lady Laura with the fireman in all his gear to punish me for playing with matches. It was amaaaaaazing! So much fun. Laura had fun being my "slutty mom," who was all over the

fireman, and I was the errant child who needed a lesson. I was as sassy as I could be when I wasn't laughing because everything was so hilarious, and we all had a blast. Being spanked by a fireman is hot! Literally.

Roleplaying was a very big deal with a lot of the clients. If you think about it, it makes perfect sense. People came to us to escape reality and play out their innermost fantasies. I was always amazed at how creative and serious the clients got into their roles. One gentleman we shall call "Mi' Lord," again frequenting The Dominion for as long as I can remember, was a very serious roleplayer. I used to see him in my submissive days and thoroughly enjoyed his dramatic flair, from being a priest fighting the succubus to being a Roman emperor with a harem of slaves. He frequented The Dominion until the doors were closed. He just loved women. It did not matter if they were thick or thin, blonde or brunette. He was fair and gave us all a chance—another great and true friend to us.

Sometimes, it was difficult to perform some of the scenes requested. Someone wanted to have a scene recreated that he saw in a movie, and it seemed a simple thing, but it was the intensity of his feelings when he described how he felt when he saw the scene that made me leery of doing the session. I never wished to disappoint anyone, so I was honest. The session was simply putting on an opera glove, but he wanted it done exactly like in the movie and expected to feel the same way he did the first time he saw it. I knew this would

not be possible to replicate, and I told him that. He did not understand and tried to talk me into it, and I told him he would never feel the same way he did the first time he saw it because he was expecting it. The session would have been a great disappointment to him, but eventually, he got it and expressed his appreciation for my honesty.

Age play was a very popular fantasy, but I eventually gave it up because it was too much psychologically for me. I learned a lot of things the hard way, and doing Daddy/daughter fantasies was just not my cup of tea for obvious reasons. However, it took me some time to figure that out, and I learned the hard way. Sometimes, if you are with someone who can really get into your head and you are vulnerable to certain triggers, you are in a danger zone. I found myself in this very situation one day at The Chateau. I saw someone who had just gone into a Daddy/daughter scene in the room without warning me. We never discussed it in the interview, but he was younger than me, so at first, I felt I would be able to handle it. But he was super intense, which caught me off-guard. I guess I was just not mentally prepared for it. I had flashbacks during the session, and I literally lost myself. He probably felt everything in our session was consensual, but Bunny had left the room a long time ago, and little Debbie entered and became the victim once again.

He would never know I felt raped because I honestly wasn't there. I had checked out mentally and was in another time, space, and dimension. It was so traumatizing that it fucked with me for a

long time. I was so ashamed that I'd never told anyone until now. I never did another age-play session for the rest of my career, and when I trained new Ladies, I always warned them about psychological triggers in session and told them to please be careful.

A good old-fashioned OTK (over-the-knee) spanking was always a great inspiration for lots of different roles: school principal disciplining someone caught smoking on the playground, a seductive student trying to get a passing grade in college, juvenile delinquent caught hitchhiking. One such spanker was our client, who called himself *'Spanking Sam.'* He deemed himself the house disciplinarian. He would call on the phone, and we had to tell him things were completely out of hand and that we needed his help. The desk mistress had to make up infractions, or we would stage arguments in the lobby so he could hear it over the phone. The Ladies were smoking weed in the back, fighting with each other, or disrespecting the desk mistress. Those were just a few of the infractions we made up. It was a lot of work for the desk person because he would ho-hum about it and call back several times before actually coming in.

When he finally showed up, we often would go to the back and pull the errant young lady in need of discipline out by her ear and hand her over with a reprimand. You really had to know how to control this one because he just spanked nonstop for 30 minutes, so if you played your cards right and put up a fight, you could save

your ass. I saw him once in the lobby in my submissive days, and there were two swivel leather chairs, which were not ideal for spanking but worked okay. I was over his lap, and I started tying his shoelaces together on his shoes. He had no clue what was going on. I just egged him on, and he carried on spanking. He did finally discover what I had done, and this produced more vigor in his swing, which somehow resulted in the chairs upending on top of us. He never stopped. It was hilarious.

We had the door open so others could see, and it turned into quite a circus. Everyone had a good laugh with it, but he took it very seriously, and I don't even know if he realized the chairs were on top of us at the end of the session because he was so into it. When he saw a sub, he would take them out to the desk and show the desk person the Lady's red bum and ask if they thought she had learned her lesson. It was always fun to play with the Ladies and tell him, "No, I don't think so. I think she needs a longer lesson." You could always see the "love/hate you" look on the Lady's face. Sam was a special person, and if he would not come in for a while, we would worry about him. Eventually, we figured out a way to check to see if he was okay to ease our minds. We knew someone who worked at the same company he did (albeit in a different department), so she was able to check on him discreetly. He was a sweet and simple man, and we cared for him a lot.

"Apple Barry" was an interesting guy to whom Lady Laura gave his name for his affinity for having produce stuck up his ass.

He was very meek and into humiliation during his session but held a position of power in the real world. He brought hours of entertainment to the Ladies with his talents, and we all loved to see him dusting with a feather duster in his ass.

"Master Britt" was a treat for most. He was a Texan who lived in Virginia and was so excited when he came in. He would arrange to see some of the Ladies before he left on his trip, but most of the Ladies knew if they said hello to him, they would be getting their bums spanked as well. There are things that happen in a BDSM environment that would never be acceptable in the outside world. They would be considered degrading to women, and that would be the case, but inside the walls of a BDSM club, it was part of the role, and most of it was harmless.

Master Britt measured the Ladies' bums by the size of his hands. The lady would be a two-hander or a 4-hander, meaning when he put his hand on you to spank you, how many hands did it take to cover your butt. One of the first things he would do in a session would be run his hands over your legs to see if you were shaved. If not, you never heard the end of it, and you would for sure shave your legs before you saw him again. Eventually, everyone caught on to the leg-shaving thing, and you could see the Ladies running around the back room looking for a razor before they saw him.

He loved all of us so much, and his happiness at being with us

was so infectious that you could not help but love him. He was very respectful of the Ladies' limits, and all he did was hand-spanking. He was like a kid in a candy store every time he came in and used to extol the virtues of The Dominion to any other clients sitting in the lobby with us. Master Britt was loved by all. We were all so sad when he developed cancer and passed away. We missed him terribly.

One of the best spanking scenes ever was a surprise arranged by a submissive for her Master. She had planned to play errant schoolgirls with five other ladies, and he would be the headmaster. The best part was that he had no idea what he was going to be walking into. The Ladies were all dressed in matching uniforms, and they looked like well-behaved schoolgirls, but once they were given the go-ahead that he was on his way up to the room, they went wild. The room was toilet-papered, and paper wads were flying amid a commotion the likes he had never witnessed before. You see, he was quite a serious Dominant, and he had played with everyone in the room before, so they were deriving a great deal of joy from the chaos of the scene and the possible repercussions of their behavior. When he opened the door, he was absolutely gobsmacked, and it took him a minute to assess the situation and, frankly, to stop laughing. This was not going to be a serious situation. The Ladies were undisciplined and rowdy, and it was a blast. Everyone still came out of it with ruby-red butt cheeks and big smiles on their faces. Cleaning the room was a bitch.

Some of the scenes were just precious and I personally felt honored that someone would share these secrets with us.

Graham was 81 years old and lived in Canada. Once or twice a year, he would come down to visit. He was adorable. He was always dressed to the nines in his bow tie and straw hat. We liked him seeing the more experienced Ladies, and that is what he did. You must take extra care of older clients, especially when they want to play hard. You had to take such care with them and watch their skin because it was so thin. It was heartbreaking to have to tell someone it was not safe for them to play as heavily as they wished, but I think they appreciated playing with someone who cared and was looking out for their best interests. A lot of Ladies were fearful of playing with him, which was understandable. He came with his own strap and only wanted six of the best. It was the most precious and touching session, and he was so dear to us.

There was an Englishman who stopped in one day to plan for a multi-hour session with four of us. The scene was very elaborate, and he supplied everything for it. He was being sent to an institution for incontinence, and we were supposed to cure him not with punishment but with kindness and words of encouragement. He was very soft-spoken and a complete gentleman who wanted to be handled with care and feel loved for a few hours. He was never to be made fun of or treated badly for this because it was an illness, but it had to be dealt with as he was a grown man. We were all dressed

as nurses, and the hospital was furnished with all manner of baby toys, diapers, and playpens. He had no plans to wet himself during the session, as that was not part of the fantasy.

I think when you play with someone on this level, it is a bonding experience, and I always felt I had helped my clients with something that they needed to deal with and had not been able to achieve in any other way. Some things are too dark in our minds to even share with a therapist. But their secrets were safe with us. I have always enjoyed the change in demeanor that happens once a session is paid for. It's like you click your fingers, and the client becomes another person before your eyes. That is part of the beauty of the escape into BDSM, becoming someone or something that you are not in a place where your secret is safe and you are not judged. You would see a client in character in session, and it would be astounding how different they were. And when they came out of session, it was business as usual and "see you next time."

One client I still remember was called "Priscilla" and she was a joy! She claimed she was not a crossdresser but a "little girl." She always came in with a note from her wife telling us she needed to be taken down a peg or two and lose some of her "macho bullshit" before she came back home. She had long hair and custom-made dresses for her play, complete with black Mary Jane shoes and white ankle socks. She was very shy and nervous but enjoyed humiliation. One of our best days was the day I put a picture of her up on the wall with the other Ladies who worked at The Dominion.

When she came in, I showed her the picture and told her to get dressed because she was going to work on the floor with the rest of us that day. She did not question me but was visibly shaken. It was great. Once she was dressed, I inspected her to make sure she was dressed properly and took her out to the lobby to "introduce" the new submissive to the Ladies. We went through all the regular information we would give a new Lady on her first day and I am certain she did not think I was going to go through with it up until the point I did. I had her sit in the lobby with the other Ladies. She was adorable. She sat with her knees together in her little, short skirt, trying to hide behind a magazine.

I did have her introduced to clients when they came in, but only clients I knew would catch on to what was going on. I told her she needed to make some money for me, so she better be charming and alluring. She trembled the entire time I had her in the room, which was for a long time. I let her have a break for lunch and put her back. She was just one of the gals that day and was the perfect submissive. She was just too damned nervous to get a session, though. She was great fun, and she came back again and again.

"Dolly Dan" was Canadian and visited two or three times a year. He did multiple hours of sessions, seeing anywhere from four to eight Ladies at a time. Everyone wanted to be one of the chosen ones, but it was a very difficult session to do. He put all the Ladies in a position, and they had to hold it for super long periods of time.

He got the "Dolly Dan" nickname because he literally was turning the Ladies into inanimate objects, and then he would spank, crop, or cane them, and they were not to move a muscle or make a sound. Sometimes, they would come out of session so cold from the lack of movement that I felt sorry for them. It was intense, but he was a generous tipper, so the longer he stayed, the happier the Ladies were when he left.

It was so interesting to know everyone's different fantasies and fetishes. Inquiring minds wanted to know where they came from and what made them tick. I personally would never ask or put them on the spot, but sometimes, they would just voluntarily tell their own stories.

A common theme for a lot of foot fetishes was either babysitters or sandals on the beach. Some people into spanking were never spanked as children and viewed a spanking as a form of love and intimacy between parent and child. Humiliation was always a rough one for me. I did not like it as a submissive or a Dominant. There are so many different kinds of humiliation, and I could roll with most of it, but when it became personal, I struggled. People could just be downright pricks. As I have mentioned before, I was not a sweet young thing when I started working. I was a single mother with three children, which left many scars of honor on my body. People who did not know what humiliation sessions were supposed to be would tell me my breasts were like cow udders and want me to moo. My hard line was making animal noises. Oinking like a pig was an

absolute no-go no matter how submissive I was, and I was a terrible puppy.

When I was playing a Dominant role while switching, I had a lovely man called Jacob who used to see me regularly. He was into Lady Marlene Merry Widows and Lily St. Cyr lingerie. *(This goes way back, so you may need to Google these items if you are curious!)* I could always tell he carried a lot of self-loathing within him, and one day in session, while I was disciplining him, he wanted me to call him a worthless piece of shit. My heart would not let me do it because I knew he felt it was true. I turned it around and told him he was insulting me because I would never waste my time on a worthless piece of shit, and if he ever said that again I would beat him mercilessly.

When the session was over, I hugged him, and he cried and thanked me. We saw each other for years after that. Several Ladies liked humiliation and were so creative with it. Sharing humiliation sessions with everyone always made it easier and a lot more fun. Having a grown man wearing a Shirley Temple dress singing "On the Good Ship Lollipop" is very entertaining and, strangely enough, could brighten up the day. It was all in good fun and never mean-spirited. The clients loved the public displays or being turned into "sissy maids" for half an hour and being forced to clean the bathrooms or kitchen for us. I always felt it was a special kind of submission, and it made them happy to do it.

I was always amazed at how much torture a penis could take once I got over the shock of seeing it. I was always amazed by ball-busting. One beloved man who looked like David Crosby *(please tell me you know who he is!)* was so much fun, and you could not wear him down. He rode a Harley and was a total biker dude who loved being kicked in the balls. There was a very specific way it had to be done, which involved him on his knees with his legs spread open and the kicker at the other end of the room to start. The most important part of the scene was the menacing walk in stilettos you had to do on the trip to reach the final destination of a big swift kick to his balls. You could see the fear in his eyes, but that was the part he loved. His legs would shake, and you could see him battling his natural reflex to save his balls, but he could not close his legs. It was a struggle for sure, and he would stay for hours sometimes. I had to admire him, and he was a great stress release!

Lady Kalleen was always coming up with strange and wonderful scenarios, and she had a client who was a truck driver who brought in a big, clunky old typewriter to hang from his balls. I always wondered what made him decide one day that he wanted a typewriter hanging from his balls, but again, I admired the scene!

Some sessions were truly specialized, and you really needed to know your stuff to handle them. One such person was Klaus. We adored him. He was a full-on masochist and scared some of the less experienced Ladies because his session was so intense. Since I was a former masochist when I started in the business, I understood the

need he had for this intense session, and I did not feel bad about doing it. I also knew how to read someone in that headspace, which is super important.

Now, this session, while intense, was anything but serious. There was laughter and teasing the entire time we played. I just adored this man. He was only into the cane which may sound dull, but he was REALLY into the cane. Part of the experience for him was the fear before each strike. There was no bondage, and he really had no discipline, so at times, there was a bit of chasing him around the room. I would normally let him know how many strikes I expected him to take, and he would think about it, talk about it, and try to negotiate himself out of it, but he would have been disappointed if I gave in. He also tried to bargain with me. He would say if he could not take ten strokes, I could cane his balls. He rarely could, which I think was part of his game because the fear of having his balls struck was such a high for him.

He loved every second of his time, and I always had a great appreciation for a true masochist. I proudly took credit for the blood on the ceiling of The Pink Room for years as a result of his session. Klaus was a bloody mess by the time the session was over, and we had to put a diaper on him before he left so he would not bleed through his clothes. There was a lot of aftercare involved afterward. He would come in for three days and then be gone for four months to heal. He was always happy and just a joyous human being when

he was with us. I miss him dearly.

Some clients liked to tell us the stories behind their kinks, but sometimes, we would try to figure out where a particular fetish came from on our own. Some were easy to figure out, but others were just downright dumbfounding, like the priest who wanted us covered in itchy materials with a full bladder.

He provided sweaters made of itchy wool or mohair, and we had to cover our bodies with the sweaters. We would have sweaters on our legs, wrapped around our bums and covering our faces and hands. He would call ahead and tell us to drink a liter of water before his arrival. Some did, most didn't. I was one of the dodos who did, and because he did not believe we did what we were told, he would have us drink another liter during the session. He tied us up, tickled us, and was very concerned for us, constantly asking if we itched or if we needed the bathroom. I just could not get my head around this one. First, he was a priest, and he came to a dungeon. Maybe it was a medieval thing, with ashes and sackcloth? Who knows!

A truly interesting session was Donovan. He was awesome! His session was basically begging us not to make him do or say things to him, which was the signal to make him do just exactly that. You had to take him as soon as he walked in the door. He usually phoned first, and then if the right phone person was on, she would tell him not to think about coming in, and sure enough, he would show up. It was pretty much a seduction if the right person was doing it.

*"Where are you, Donovan?"*

*"At work."*

*"Are you alone?"*

*"No, my secretary is here."*

*"Is she wearing stockings?"*

*"OOOH, don't make me think about it!"*

*"I'm wearing stockings myself, Donovan…"*

*"OOOOOOOOOHHHH."*

Fifteen minutes later, he would show up. It was a hoot, locking his hands in your garters while backing him up against the wall. He couldn't escape. He was the weakest man in the world! Fantasies were wild… One day, I made him drive me to In-N-Out Burger with his hands cuffed and his cock rope-tied to the steering wheel. The rope was around his balls and long and thin enough to have it discreetly coming out from the zipper in his trousers. His voice was shaking when he ordered the food, and when he had to turn the

steering wheel, you could hear a helpless moan come out of his mouth.

On the way back, we stopped at a liquor store, and I made him go in to buy cigarettes with his handcuffs on. So many good times. It took a lot of training to get all the Ladies on board and ready for him when he came in. Normally, we would bring another Lady into the session and show them how to deal with "the weakest man in the world." He was a wonderful session, but as time passed and the Old Timers began to phase out, it was harder and harder to get Ladies interested in his session, and he could feel the lack of interest when he came in. It saddened me when he stopped coming in, but I understood why. No one could be bothered.

Things were changing in the scene and not all of it for the better. Not all clients were joyous to be around. There were a lot of clients who felt we were glorified prostitutes and just came in to try to get a hand job. If we asked them in their interview what they were into and they could not produce an answer, we generally did not see them unless we felt they were teachable.

There were some clients who could just get under your skin walking in the door with their misogyny or bad attitudes. Some sessions I was very uncomfortable with and was not keen on the Ladies doing, but it was not my choice, it was the Ladies'.

One such man was "Lipstick Louie." He was arrogant, but not in a good way. He was the guy who threw the money on the desk

rather than hand it to you. His thing was bringing in the cheapest red lipstick he could find and writing with it on the Ladies' bodies. This was not a cool '60s body painting… it was scrawling words like "slut," "whore," "worthless," and whatever else would cross his mind to demean the Lady. Some of it was so vile that I forbade him to do it, and I eventually kicked him to the curb. It took forever for the Ladies to recover from the session. They had to shower and scrub off the lipstick, but the emotional toll those words took on them was not so easily washed away. As I said before, I normally did not interfere with the Ladies doing whatever sessions they liked, but once in a while, I just had to.

When I first started in the business, there was a notorious old man who circulated the club scene whose client name was "Ogre." He was just an angry old man, and his thing was using a cane. He had no finesse with it but knew where it could do the most damage. I saw him a couple of times back when I was a super masochist, and his favorite thing to do was cane your hands. Now, please understand that if the same session were done in a different way with a caring Dom who knew what he was doing and how to handle a submissive, it would have been a completely different session. But he was intolerable. I was very happy to see the back of him. Don't let the dungeon door hit you in the ass!

# ABSURDLY NORMAL

There were many times I was approached to allow cameras in The Dominion to film what goes on behind the scenes when we were not in session. While there were many lucrative propositions to step inside the inner sanctum of The Dominion, I would never compromise our reputation for discretion and a safe space for the mighty dollar. But I can totally understand why someone would want to film us, though. Often, the most interesting things happened in the break room or just when the Ladies hung out together.

I've mentioned before the sisterhood that forms when working in the dungeon together, and many of the Ladies formed life-long friendships. The tight bonds that developed between these women were special, unlike anything they would ever share with anyone else in their lives. But that being said, I had watched enough trash TV to know I would never subject The Dominion to the cameras under any circumstances. There was no way we would ever be shown in a positive light. I learned this from seeing Ladies do interviews on talk shows in the past. No matter what positive message the Ladies were trying to put out there, they were sensationalized and made the object of public ridicule. No one wanted to know the positive effect we had on people and the difference we made in our clients' lives. They wanted a freak show. There were other things to consider as well, including the privacy of

our clientele and the discretion in the neighborhood. So, the answer was never a second thought. Thanks, but no thanks!

One of the things I loved the most was seeing the Ladies working together to hone their craft during slow periods. The Vault was the home of so much learning and work. When I would sit at the desk, I felt a sort of motherly pride when I would see the Ladies come out to the equipment wall and gather equipment to practice on each other. One of the most important parts of BDSM is the training that senior staff gives to the newbies who are trying to learn. It used to be considered part of your responsibility as a Mistress or Switch to help with the "kids," as we called them, even though they were consenting adults.

This was how you learned, and passing the torch was imperative to continue safety and excellence in play. But as BDSM became more popular and mainstream, more and more people had no clue when they came to work for us. They hadn't done their research like so many of us had done in the past. As a result, I noticed as time passed, it became harder and harder to get senior staff to help with training. There were a few Ladies to whom all of this fell, and it really was not fair to them to have to train every new person who came in. It would kind of burn them out, and I really could not blame them.

Slow days could be a nightmare for moods. I always felt responsible or bad when the days were slow, but I also told the

Ladies not to spend all the money they made on a good day because the next week might be slow. You just never could tell.

When the Ladies got bored, it could go either way… moody or crazy. Lady Francesca, my dear and trusted friend who was also my manager and used to be known as "Gina" when we were young subs, used to get the brunt of boring days. We, too, had our share of slow times, and those were the days you would find us having a tug of wars with our nipple chains or stacking phone books on top of them for bragging rights. I was the boss, so the other Ladies were not as open to me as they were to her. They liked to torment her for some reason, which was all in good fun, but sometimes it was just too much.

There was no one better on the desk than Lady Francesca. The clients loved her; she put up with a lot from the Ladies, and she was as honest as they come. She wanted everyone to make money when they came in, and she did her best to make that happen. She had the patience of a saint sometimes, and I don't know how she did it. She worked hard. The clients were disappointed on the days she was not at the desk. She spent a lot of time talking with them and making them feel at home, and she was truly interested in them if they wanted to talk. We always told each other that when one of us went, the other would too because we could not run the place without the other person. In the end, that is exactly what happened.

Some of the goings-on at the dungeon would seem shocking to

people outside of the dungeon, but they were just everyday normal things for us. It was lovely. No one gave a second thought to coming into work to find a man dressed in a maid's outfit cleaning the toilets or opening a closet door to find a slave who had been exiled there for one reason or another. I was shocked when I was a newbie at some things, like walking into the bathroom and finding a man laid out on the floor with his head in a box because he was there to be a toilet for the day. *(Yes, that actually happened!)*

I remember one night, a bunch of frat guys had rented a bachelor party bus to take their new pledges around the city for some sort of hazing ritual. A few of the pledges were turned over to us so we could give them a proper paddling with the fraternity paddles they'd brought with them. Everyone watched, and it was great fun. The best part was when a couple of them came back at a later date and became great clients!

One day, we had a man dressed as SpongeBob drive up in his convertible and visit us. It was hilarious and joyful. People came in dressed as pirates and court jesters. Before iPhones, we had priests, rabbis, movie stars, and politicians who came in for sessions. You just never knew what the day would bring. I was always so proud that these people felt safe coming to our dungeon. Trusting that you and your secrets are safe with someone was vital to being comfortable and free in your session. The Ladies who worked then were aware of this, and no one was ever outed for coming to visit

us.

The holidays were fun because they gave us themes to work on during our sessions. Dressing subs up like New Year's Babies or Valentine's Cupid made things more fun, and we could get creative. There was even an Easter crucifixion every year for one man who was so overcome by the beauty of the adoration of Jesus that he wanted to try and feel that. It went on for hours, and it was serious business. I remember there were giant Easter Bunnies hopping around with bright red bottoms, too.

Birthdays were a big deal because the subbies wanted those birthday spankings, and it could be a very lucrative day for them. When my birthday came around, I could feel the stress over it because I used to feel the same way when Lady Laura's birthday came around. One of the most beautiful gifts I ever received was the honor of Switch Sky singing to me. She is an opera singer, and when she sang to me, it, of course, made me cry. The Ladies did some wonderful things for me, and I treasure those memories.

Christmas was always special to us, and not just because we could do Christmas-tree-light bondage in sessions! Seeing Ladies in their gear helping Lady Laura wrapping Christmas gifts for her grandchildren or wrapping gifts for other holidays was not uncommon. One of the Ladies who worked with us, named Kim, used to do a lovely thing for underserved kids during the holidays. She had a couple of Harleys. One had dildos painted all over it,

which shocked me to no end when I saw it in the driveway of our building one day. (So much for discretion!) She used to take toys to the kids on her other age-appropriate Harley every year at Christmas. She dressed like Santa Claus and just drove around town passing out toys to kids she would see. Lady Laura used to make Grasshoppers for us at Christmas time. It was the only time we could drink at work, and it was just as well. One night, I had Lady Laura's Grasshoppers; I was laid out on the floor next to the desk, flinging canes and crops while crying for no reason. I was never a good drinker!

And if one of the Ladies was getting married, watch out! We went all out. Bachelorette parties were over the top, and I recall one bridal shower that involved crossdressers with beards and male strippers hanging upside-down in straight jackets. Expect the unexpected!

There were so many amazing and talented women who came through the doors of The Dominion, from a punk rock schoolteacher who taught disadvantaged children to someone who worked in the District Attorney's office. We had opera singers, policewomen, college students, moms, and grandmothers working with us. I even once interviewed a Royal who was interested in joining us *(I promise!)*, but I was not too keen on the potential paparazzi problems that would come with that. *I am sworn to secrecy on this one, so don't ask!*

One woman named "Mistress Danielle," who worked with us miraculously, had incredible plumbing skills, and that made her a Superwoman in our eyes. The plumbing was not great in the building, and having forty to fifty women working at the dungeon did put some stress on the plumbing for sure. Mistress Danielle would dress up for us when the toilets or sinks needed help. Sometimes, I thought people may have deliberately clogged things up just to see the stunning beauty in her Daisy Dukes and fishnets, as well as her wife-beater shirt and hard hat. Add the black stilettos, and it was perfection.

Some people think women get into BDSM work because they have no other options in life, which couldn't be further from the truth. It was always so offensive to us when a client wanted to "rescue us" from our fate. I never in all the years I worked met a woman who was not there by choice. It is the perfect job for anyone who is into it because it allows you a flexible schedule where you make a decent amount of money, and you call the shots on what you do. We were not victims, nor were we bad people.

Along with the people who wanted to save us who came in once in a while, we would get a group of people who decided it was their duty to bring us to the Lord… once again, assuming we were all sinners and in league with the devil. The funny thing about these people is they were not very Christian in their approach to us, and their only goal was to shut us down (after they had sessioned there, of course). One group (and I will not name the religious affiliation)

threatened to picket us in front of our building, and they did. We had a news crew in front of the building, and it was pretty terrifying but more annoying than anything. This is when an expensive lawyer is a must-have. He handled everything for us and made the problem disappear. It was a very short protest!

There was a lovely woman who had worked for me for years, and we were very close friends. She was a teacher, and eventually, she decided to leave the dungeon and go independent, but we remained friends. Since we were no longer working together, we did not see much of each other, and when we did, she was making some huge changes to her life. One day, she told me she was marrying a pastor. I was very happy for her, and it actually seemed the perfect life for her if you knew her like I did.

She was a very 1950s housewife type with never a hair out of place. Once she was married, I didn't see much of her, but I found when I did, she was trying to "save me," so I just quietly bowed out of the relationship. I do have my own faith, and I never understood why people just assume you don't if you're in this business. One night, I got a phone call from the person on the desk to let me know that some women were at the front door and that my friend (the pastor's wife) had sent them with some gifts for the Ladies. I permitted her to let them in. This turned out to be another attempt to save the poor sex workers who were trapped into working in this horrible club.

They left little bags with cheap lipstick and earrings in them and a card with an outreach number in it if we needed help. I was livid and insulted. This woman had been here for years and knew everything about this business, and to imply that the women working for me needed help was beyond the pale for me. They continued to come in on a monthly basis. It seems they make the rounds to strip clubs and other sex work establishments. I finally put the kibosh on it and told them they were not welcome but that we appreciated their prayers.

# LADY BOSS

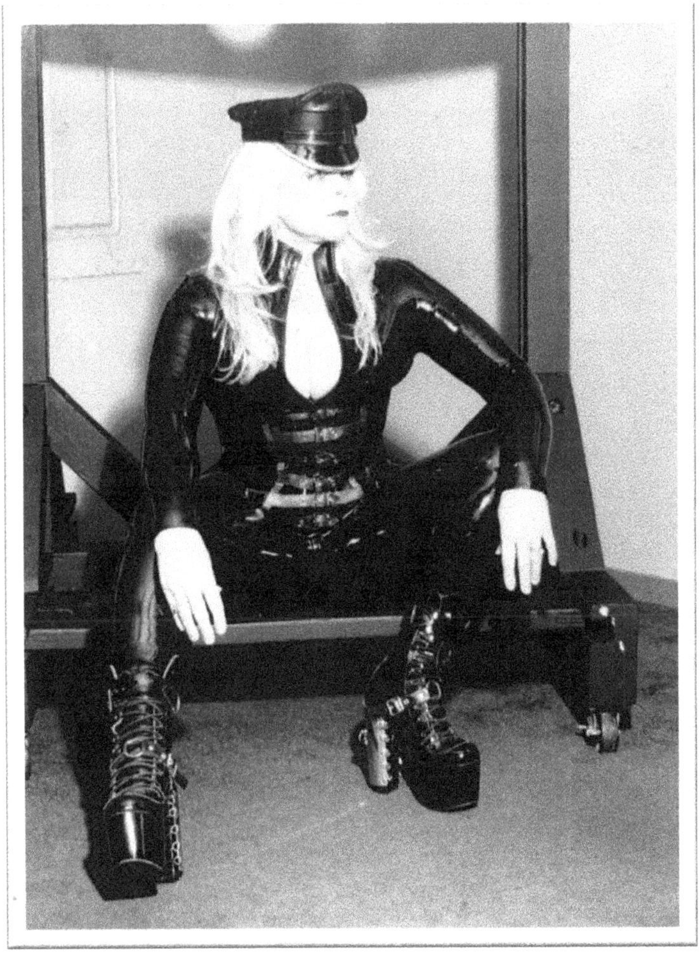

I was honored and blessed that Lady Laura left me her Dominion. This was a huge life-changing moment for me. I had

spent my life in a repressed state of mind with no self-confidence, and this Lady trusted me with her legacy. I was determined to get things back on the right track and make Lady Laura the shining star of the BDSM community. I kept the name Lady Laura's Dominion for five years before I felt that it was mine. After that, I just called it The Dominion.

What always saddened me deeply was once I became "the boss," my relationships changed with a lot of my friends. There was, of course, the original anger and jealousy of me being "given" Lady Laura's with all the joys that would bring me and, of course, all the money I would make. And as time went on, distance grew when rules were not bent, or disagreements arose on how I wanted to run my Dominion. I was left with a lot of things that were very difficult for me to manage. Please keep in mind that I am submissive by nature. I am strong, for sure, but non-confrontational, so it took me a long time to "bend" people to my will.

Eventually, this meant having an entirely new crew of people working with me. Things had always been a little loosey-goosey in the houses in the '80s and '90s, but we never had any trouble with police because we were legit. The only people messing with us really were other club owners and their minions. My nature has always been to do things right, and you never have to worry, so that was how I needed things to be for this to work for me.

One of the first things I needed to do was get some of the

obnoxious, annoying men out of the building who contributed nothing and felt that they could bully me. They were hangers-on and contributed nothing to The Dominion. One such person was a self-professed "gypsy" who had a slave working for Lady Laura and now me. She was especially loosey-goosey and was not keen on changing her behavior. He would sit in the lobby the entire time she was working and make comments along with his troll friend, and because they were men, they thought they were running the show. I had a habit of making sure at night that all the Ladies made it out to their cars safely. Making sure the Ladies were safe was my responsibility.

For some reason, this made him angry, and he lit into me. I am sure there was more to it than that. His slave had come to me earlier and asked me to help her in a session. A client wanted to pierce her nipple, and she was not comfortable with him doing it, so she asked me if I would, and I agreed so that she would be safe. When her Master found out, he was incensed. Not my problem. This was his last night at The Dominion. I did not need his abuse, nor was I going to accept any abuse from anyone inside the sanctum of The Dominion.

I became the enforcer. I had set rules in place to protect the staff, and it was not an easy change for some, especially for some of the clients who had been around since Lady Laura's day. I remember how powerless I felt at times in a session as a submissive because

there weren't rules in place to protect me. That's why it was very important to me that the people who worked with me felt a sense of empowerment and that they called the shots in their sessions. I made sure they did not have to do anything they did not wish to do and that they knew I would back up their decisions.

As I mentioned earlier, the rule that got the most flack was the G-string/thong rule. We did not have a nudity license, nor did any BDSM club at the time, so nudity was not something we should have been offering in the first place. The Ladies were fine with it. It was so much easier to keep hands away from places they should not be when they were covered up. Clients complained they could not do a bare-bottom spanking, which was ludicrous since your bottom cannot get much more bare than in a G-string or thong.

The Ladies became very creative. For every argument, there was a solution to the problem. Spankers who wanted to pull down their panties to spank could still do so because the Ladies would wear a thong under the panties. They were very adaptable. For those special clients who liked to surprise you by disrespecting your limits and pulling your thong down… it was magic. Most of the Ladies took to wearing two or three at a time. Eventually, everybody got the idea that this would remain the status quo and learned how to spank and still enjoy the experience on the lovely cheeks that were molded by the wearing of the thong.

I remember when I was one of the staff, so many times clients

would give me the old wink-and-nod *"Well, you know Lady Laura and I go way back"* story, which they felt entitled them to special favors. It was the same for the Ladies when I became the boss. Like I mentioned earlier, I had an easy fix. I just used to tell them to tell the client that I would be happy to give him that blow job after I asked Lady Hillary or called her at home. "If she says it is okay, I will do it." I never got any of those phone calls, but I heard the stories later. It was effective. Unfortunately, there were times when I had to "86" clients. We had a list of people who were either very disrespectful to the Ladies, violated Ladies in session, were violent or stalkers, and were expelled from The Dominion forever. I would never have had any problem calling the police for help and I did indeed do so a couple of times. This was one of the bonuses of running my business legally. There was no thinking twice about it if we needed help.

If I was not there, the Ladies knew that if they invoked my name, I would back them up. Sometimes clients would want to session with me, and I could no longer do it because I did not feel it was right to take the money away from the other Ladies. This was one reason, and the other was that I was working six to seven days a week. You are never off when you are the boss. It is kind of like when I tried to explain to clients who wanted 24/7 slave relationships. The fantasy is always so much better than the reality of it. Once it becomes the norm, it is just that.

I hated that I was no longer one of the girls. I maintained a few close friends over the years, but most of them go way back. We are the Old Timers, the trailblazers, the forgotten ones, the badasses that made BDSM what it is today. We gave submissives a voice and women a voice in BDSM.

I always felt the Ladies cared for me and I suppose they did in a different way. Once I was the boss, I could feel the hush in the room when I would enter and noticed people did not confide in me like they used to. It was hurtful. I wanted the best for everyone. I did feel very protective of them and I did have a ridiculously big heart at one time. I had my own personal struggles in my life, as we all do, but when someone who worked for me was in trouble or needed a hand, I would do it. I think this is why, as time went on, when I owned the business, I became more distant from the staff. I always had trust issues, and yet I still trusted, which was detrimental to me most of the time. I cannot remember why, but I had two Ladies living in my home with myself and my new husband. I am pretty sure it was because they were being evicted or something of that nature.

One of them was my submissive, so it was a given I would help her. She moved in first, and shortly after her, the "house fairy" moved in. She was a lovely girl, but she lived in her own world, and sometimes, I was sure she was from another planet. These arrangements always start out with "until I can get on my feet," which, in retrospect, is pretty open-ended and a terrible contract. But

I was the optimistic sort. I never really minded having other people living with us at first. But eventually, I started becoming the "asshole in the relationship" by making "unreasonable" demands on those living with me to maybe clean their bathroom or wash their dishes. One of the women was an artist, and my husband schlepped her around town to help her sell her art. We also helped buy her a car and ate that. I never made them move out. Just waited for my guardian angel above to do her work and fix the situation for me, and after more than a year's time, it eventually happened.

The worst was a girl named Violet, who I had great affection for and who had worked for me for years. She came and went, and I liked her a lot, as did the Ladies. She had been with me for years. I, of course, did not know that she had a drug problem. I did detect strange behavior one night when she was coming out of session and stumbling in the lobby, and I asked her about it. She told me she was seeing a therapist and taking some medication for depression that was messing with her. Sounded fair to me.

Time passed, and she needed a place to stay for one reason or the other. And I had a spare room at my house, so I offered it to her temporarily. She even met my grandchildren and my children while staying with me. After she had gone back home to St. Louis to visit family for the holidays, I got a phone call to bail her out of jail for possession. That flipped a switch in me that I never knew I had. I felt like such an idiot. I told her no and forbade her from coming

back to my house ever again. I offered to pack up her stuff and take it somewhere that she could get it.

Packing her things was a real eye-opener. She had crack pipes under the bed and was using my grandchild's sippy cup as an ashtray. I had a bunch of my daughter's clothes packed away in the room Violet was staying in, which apparently she helped herself to.

I have been kind and have done my best to lend a hand to those who needed it. But no good deed goes unpunished. I've been met with such vitriol at times, and it just became too much. But thankfully, not everyone took advantage of me like Violet did. There was at least one person I could still trust. Thank God for Francesca!

# TOGETHER FOR THE DURATION

Francesca and I were pals when we started in the business, and then it seemed we ended up in parallel universes at times. It seemed that she was always a step ahead of me when working at other clubs. She left Lady Laura's and eventually ended up at the Chateau and then Passive Arts. She was very good friends with a then mutual friend of ours who I fell out with over time, but it did not affect our relationship. I just did not see her much when she worked at other clubs. I always considered her a dear friend. We had called ourselves "slave sisters" in our early days, and it has carried through to this day. I love her dearly, and there is nothing I would not do for her if it were in my power.

I was always a little envious of her when she was "Submissive Gina." She was so tiny and adorable, and everyone loved her. My perspective was that she was confident in who she was and what she had to offer, smart, and knew her value as a person and a submissive. She had a gift of gab that I never had. I was very withdrawn and probably gave the impression I was not interested in people because I was not a great conversationalist. In contrast, Gina could just engage anyone and know their life story before they left and remember it when they came back to see her. She was an excellent

submissive, and we were very competitive. To this day, I tease her that I was the submissive who got my ass beat, and she was the sub who "cutesy-ied" her way out of everything with her adorable baby voice.

This, of course, was not fair because she could hold her own in a scene for sure. I was just more stubborn. There came a point in time when working the floor was not what Gina wanted to do, and she began working reception as Francesca at another club. This did not work out for her, so she came to me, and I gladly accepted the blessing of having Francesca on my team.

It was not long before Francesca was the manager of The Dominion. She worked hard and was trustworthy, and for the first time, I felt I truly had someone who had my back. The Ladies loved her, and the clients did as well. With Francesca there, I eventually felt comfortable enough to put more of the day-to-day running of the business in her hands. She shielded me from a lot of the petty bullshit, which would really rile me up at times, or she'd run interference with some of the crazy goings-on between the Ladies that I could do without. She knew all my fragilities and protected me as much as she could from the cruelties of the business at times. I could never have imagined a better friend, and I am grateful to still have her in my life today.

# 8871

Despite the lack of faith that the naysayers had in me, the dungeon was thriving. Scheduling appointments had to be done carefully, and at times, we had to run things with military accuracy. If we saw the appointment books were full at the beginning of the day, we would let the Ladies know they needed to be ready to go and not waste time getting out of the rooms. We were not keen on rushing people out of session, but there were times we had to, or someone would lose a session, which was just not fair. Most people respected this, and we always did our best to accommodate "shit happens" situations, but for those who were just habitually late or inconsiderate, we sometimes had to cut their time short to be fair to the others waiting. It was a subtle punishment that worked and could not be argued.

We had a total of four rooms in the building in addition to the interview room. Most people always wanted the upstairs rooms. As fate would have it, there was a building next door with a parking lot that had been empty for a year. It had been sold before we even knew it was for sale. For years, my accountant had owned the building. One day, a realtor came knocking on the door to let us know they were going to be building apartment buildings with underground parking right up next to our building. As far as I was concerned, that would have been our demise.

205

My husband Robert is a master negotiator, and in July of 2008, we ended up with the building ourselves, which was such a major blessing. Never dreamed this would even be an option and have a parking lot, too! The possibilities were endless now. I was able to put my creative hat back on and design five more dungeons. This was going to be such a help, and we would be able to accommodate more clients and more Ladies. It was perfect.

I always enjoyed creating the rooms. Mistress Crystal helped me a lot. She did most of the heavy work, and she designed the beautiful Bastille Room, which always blew my mind. We were now able to add to the room roster: The Bettie Page Room for domestic scenes; The Sanctum, with its beautiful iron cross; Detention, a small school room; and The Enclave, which was a spacious room that featured all the dungeon furniture you could want.

We called the new building The Annex, and it was a godsend once it was done. Most of the dungeon furniture was made by a man we called "Downtown Willy." Willy was well-known in the scene and also did terrific metalwork. He is still working to this day. His work is impeccable, and I would highly recommend him to anyone. All the rooms were elegant and comfortable. Everyone wanted to go to The Annex now.

It was always important to me to make sure the equipment was kept up and that we had plenty of toys for everyone to play with. It

was important to me because I personally learned the difference in how I carried myself when I had a beautiful space to play in and equipment that was nice. It is the same as being dressed appropriately. The first time I put on leather before a Domme session, I likened it to slipping into a different skin, and I could feel the change inside as the leather encased my body. Cinching up my corset and zipping up my thigh-high boots were all part of the ritual of play for me. It was very important to my performance as a Domina, just as wearing the correct attire as a submissive just put me in the right headspace.

It used to drive me insane trying to get some of the Ladies to understand the importance of the gear. First, I felt that for the money clients were paying for a session (which was up to $160 an hour at that time), they deserved all that BDSM had to offer, which included fetish wear. To be fair, sometimes clients liked street clothes, and that was part of the fantasy for them. Lots of spankers appreciated this.

When I discovered the joy of latex, that was it for me; I loved the way it hugged my curves, as did the clients. I even used to like it when I wasn't playing anymore, because I was the boss who got to get dressed up and sit at the desk. It was a lesson of sorts to some of the Ladies that clothes can make the woman. I so enjoyed turning down session requests while dressed to the nines behind the desk. It was great for my ego and good for the youngsters to see that there

is more to BDSM than being young and beautiful and giving someone the privilege of your company because you are just all that.

*The Enclave*

*The Sanctum*

208

*The Bastille*

*The Equipment Room*

# THE "KIDS" GROW UP

I have previously mentioned how much I loved being a Dungeon Mother. I think it is a truly important responsibility to help young women learn the art of BDSM in a safe and sane environment while inspiring them to speak up for themselves and be in control of their well-being while working. I, of course, had many special attachments with some women who just stole my heart when we met. The wonderful thing about working in a house is the safety it offers to those who wish to learn the art, and the friendships some of the Ladies form with each other last a lifetime.

I was very protective of new submissives and wanted them appropriately trained. While many protested that they even had to be submissive in the first place, it was the "Old School" way of doing things, and I agreed with it 100%. It was a rocky road for some who did not have a submissive bone in their bodies, but I always appreciated their effort and desire to learn the right way. I am certain that most of them today who are now preeminent Dominas in the community view their submissive time as an important part of the process and their growth to becoming good Dommes.

I am still proud of the women who went out on their own and blazed a path for themselves in the community. They were very hands-on and helpful with outside events as a spokesperson for The Dominion.

I was always sad when the Ladies left. They started as young women exploring and wanting to learn, and I was able to watch them grow up and bloom in their power. It always hurts when my BDSM babies grow up and leave the nest, but it is just like being a mother. You experience the pride of doing the best you can to give them the tools to succeed… and boy, have they succeeded!

Not everyone was a fan of mine. I was very set in my ways because it was my recipe for success, and I had proven that it worked. Sometimes Ladies would come in and interview, and we would go over everything that would be expected of them to be a member of The Dominion family. But once they started, they would be offended by pretty much anything that was asked of them. Most of these Ladies were not seriously into BDSM but were instead looking to make a quick buck and wanted to be a Dominant shortly after they started. They had no respect for the process because they did not get it, so they would not last long. A client once affectionately called them "tourists," which I thought was a perfect description of the situation. It never took long for them to leave, which was good for all sides.

I tried very hard to be fair and objective with everyone who worked with me, but sometimes, Ladies who had been with me for a long time would turn on me for things that I really did not have any control over. It was always heartbreaking for me when someone I loved lied about me or spread ugly rumors or just "fake news-ed"

me for their own personal agendas. One thing I always prided myself on was my honesty both to the clients and to the Ladies who worked for me. Sometimes, they just could not take responsibility for their actions, and I became the whipping boy. I never expected everyone to like me, and I did not like everyone who worked for me either, but I was fair, and actually, if I did not care for someone, I was normally more patient with them because I really wanted to be fair. I just wanted to have their respect as the Lady of the House and a mentor.

I am very proud of the opportunities I was able to afford the women who worked with me. The Dominion offered a safe space where you could be your own person and call your own shots in session. There were rules, of course, because in BDSM, there are protocols that need to be followed. I really loved the way I was brought up in the scene, but some very exploitative situations went on. When working for men, sometimes your feelings were not a consideration in their decision-making.

While I was submissive when I started and enjoyed serving Masters, sometimes their cruelty or thoughtlessness was shocking to me. It took me a long time to discover my self-worth, and when I ran The Dominion, I never wanted any of the Ladies who worked with me to feel undervalued or like a commodity. I know there are a lot of different views and opinions on how I did. I could feel it sometimes when I walked into the building, a kind of undercurrent or weird vibe if I had to make a rule change because common sense

did not prevail in a situation where I thought it should. I always assumed everyone was a grown-up or really cared about working there.

Some of the time, people were very enthusiastic when they started, and as time went on, they became jaded or lazy and did not want to work as a family unit, which was my expectation, and they just became bitter and not good to have around. In an environment where you have so many people in a small space, discontent spreads very quickly and is detrimental to all the reasons we were there. You cannot work in a toxic environment when you are supposed to be dealing with other people's emotions and needs.

The Dominion was a beautiful tapestry of differences. When someone had a rough day or did not make money, it was hard and difficult to keep a positive attitude alive. We all experienced it. Clients always wanted to see the new shiny girls. Most of the time, it was because they thought they would be able to get away with more if they saw a new Lady. It was typical to make really good money when you first started and then dip when someone new came in or after you had been there a couple of months. We always tried to warn the Ladies that this was a possibility, but it never felt good when it happened. Then there were the Ladies who were just so damned beautiful and young and talented that they rocked the house every time they came to work, which would be soul-destroying for some of the Ladies who did not have all of that going on for them.

Believe me, I experienced it.

There were the senior staff who had developed relationships with their clients over the years and garnered the devotion of these men and did well. When I was on the floor, I knew how good I was and was always dressed to the nines, but it did not always matter how good you were. This was a constant source of frustration when I was working as a sub because, in those days, the rules were ignored a lot by some of the Ladies, and they cleaned up financially.

There was never any point in talking to the person running the house because they were making money, too, and they always blamed it on our jealousy. Those of us who experienced this just wanted a level playing field, which was one reason I never turned a blind eye to clients asking for special favors. First, they were not mine to give, and it felt so demeaning to me when I experienced these situations. I always told the Ladies that if anyone told you that they were a friend of mine, alarm bells should go off and that they were not expected to break any rules on my behalf.

As the years went on, I had Lady Francesca managing The Dominion for me. This allowed me more time outside of the dungeon, and this was both a good thing and a bad thing. It was not healthy for me to be there seven days a week, and frankly, I knew

the Ladies liked working with Francesca, and The Dominion was in her safe hands. The bad part of this was that I grew further apart from the Ladies, and I hardly knew them at times.

It was sad for me. I am still saddened when I think about how much I loved some of these women, but I had to keep them at arm's length for my own sanity. The more times I was hurt, the more fragile I became mentally, so protecting myself was super important. It was not my ideal or the way I wanted to be, but when you are an empath, sometimes hearing everyone's troubles or just feeling the vibe in a room can suck the life out of you. I knew I had to slow down. I certainly was not getting any younger, and I had a beautiful new life with Sir Robert that I wanted to live.

# THE JOY OF SURRENDER

*Dungeon Bunny*

It is such a joyous and intoxicating experience to be able to surrender yourself completely to another human being. To feel that you can trust someone with your physical and mental well-being and not have to worry about yourself but just "be" is an amazing experience. The connection that is formed between two people who can do this is one that will never be broken or forgotten. I have a lot of little pieces of my submissive heart that belong to amazing Dominants because they took that with them when they left.

As a submissive, your first instinct is to trust the Dom you are with, and this is not always a good idea. I always trusted very quickly, and this did not always bode well for me. I am mostly referring to client relationships. With more experience, I eventually learned that I could not give all of myself to just anyone who came in to do a session. Most real submissives want to be able to go into "subspace" when they play, but that was something I had to turn off in a session unless I was with a long-trusted Master.

Subspace is when you lose yourself in session, and your brain gets foggy like you are high. Your pain tolerance is higher, and that's why it is so dangerous to go into subspace in a paid session since a submissive could easily get hurt. It's kind of like not operating heavy machinery when you are drunk! I have to admit, I became a bit of a snob when it came to who I wanted to give that special part of myself to. I am certain it is part of the growing experience.

There comes a time in one's sub career where it is difficult to give the respect every Dom who walks in the door thinks he is due. I preferred playing with older or experienced Doms. If I was not a happy sub in session, I turned smartass and dared the Dom to do something about it. I was lucky because my ass could cash the check I was writing when it came to this game. I had to have a strong Dominant because I was such a strong submissive.

Not all connections are immediate. Sometimes, it takes patience and time for relationships to form, and if you did not see someone on a regular basis, it was more difficult to cultivate these relationships and figure each other out.

Thus was the relationship with my Sir Robert (formerly known as "Scottish Bob.") He lived in England and did not visit often. I was his first session ever, and he was such a gentleman that he could not bring himself to hurt me. A little sassy brat submissive could fix that easily, though. When he visited me, he always made me feel so special, and the more we saw each other, the closer we became. He was not a Dom who knew everything or who didn't want any help learning. Sir wanted to learn the mechanics of BDSM, so that was very important to him.

What he needed no help with was his effect on me when I saw him. I would get so excited when I knew he was coming to visit, and our sessions always seemed too short. It became gut-wrenching after a while for us to part. We used to just sit and hold each other, hoping

to get enough of one another to hold us over until the next time we met. He felt the same way. He used to tell me he would just sit in his car because he was unable to drive once we parted. He was so great with the psychological aspect of play that there were times he never had to lift a piece of equipment to have me jumping and terrified. I loved mental games, and he was a natural!

There was a time I was expecting him to visit and was told that he would not be able to get to me because something had come up, but he was sending his best friend in for a session with me instead, and I had better not disappoint. His friend's name was Richard, and he was into horses. It did not take me long to figure out my plan for our session. I would be a pony. Fortunately, I had enough time to prepare and get what I needed to pull this off. I ordered horse hoofs (all four feet) from Australia that were beautiful and made a lovely clumpy sound when you walked in them. I bought a harness and a bridle and made myself a very obnoxious feathered headdress.

I was very nervous about our meeting. I was to be taken up to our room (The Chamber) and wait for Richard's arrival, blindfolded and bent over a spanking horse. And so it was. I followed directions to the tee. Lady Olivia had the job of taking me to the room and putting me into position. We were in the room for minutes, and I could hear the slow, deliberate footsteps on the stairs coming up to the room. I was so scared. What if he was an asshole and nothing like Robert? I was prepared for anything. As I promised, I would not

disappoint Sir Robert.

The door slowly opened, which was easy to figure out by the lovely creaking sound it always made. I could feel the anxiety Olivia was experiencing, hoping all went well. Silence. This was a game I had played many times but on the other side, I could feel his presence in the room and the movement of him walking around me as if inspecting his new horseflesh. Still no words, just silence. I could feel him watching me. I tried not to squirm and then it happened. I felt His touch. He just ran his fingers from the bottom of my ass to the top. It was my Sir. I knew it as soon as he touched me.

I had the audacity to speak meekly and sputtered out the word "Sir?" It was a beautiful moment that I shall never forget. Lady Olivia was dismissed and I was later told how much that moment moved her. He took off my blindfold and we embraced each other so passionately. He was taken aback a bit that I knew his touch from all the others I had felt in my time. His was the touch that mattered, that reached into my soul and my heart every time I felt it. The touch of my Sir … there was nothing sweeter!

# MY KNIGHT IN SHINING ARMOR

There are many layers to me and Sir Robert's love story. When we met, he was separated, and I was still married to M, so we kept our relationship on a professional level, but we both knew IT was there. My marriage to M was falling apart because he did not keep the promises of our BDSM relationship, which I needed to have in a marriage. Even though he was 6,000 miles away, Sir Robert filled me with all I ever dreamed of as a submissive. He was kind, charming as hell, creative, and could see into my soul. Combine that with a sexy Scottish accent, and what more could a girl ask for?

Not long after My Lady passed, M and I called it quits. My children were all grown now, and I was on my own. Sir helped me find a place near work, which made things so much easier. I loved my new apartment, and since I would be alone, he arranged for the manager to look after me while he was gone. He was so protective of me, and I had never experienced that in my life. I am a romantic and always wanted a man who would fight for my honor if need be, and he was that man. I felt like I had entered some kind of sexy fairytale and felt like a silly schoolgirl around him. I had decided in my own mind that I would be his slave for life, no matter what the situation was for him. Our sessions were so intense… not so much

pain-wise, though that would come later as our relationship progressed. It became emotionally devastating for me every time he had to leave. Him giving me homework was a great distraction. I loved sitting at the desk writing down lines, and if I goofed, I had to start all over, and I did.

I wrote him letters. So many letters! I am much better at expressing my feelings on paper than verbally, and I know to this day that we fell in love via our letters to each other. I feel sorry for the generation that will never know the joy of getting a letter from someone. Something as simple as shopping for writing paper could be an all-day project. I used to look for special paper with matching envelopes and even went as far as having a box of sealing wax. I love rituals, and letter-writing was no exception. I can make anything an event!

The anticipation of him coming into town was so exciting… from planning the outfit I would wear to the airport to pick him up, to how I would set up the room for our session. I think I have always been a bit of an exhibitionist. I liked turning heads and shocking people even more, so going to the airport in the long black leather trench coat and six-inch platform heels with lingerie underneath was a no-brainer. You don't even have to see people looking at you, but you can feel it. I always walked with pride and defiance, enjoying the reactions of people to the way I looked. Most would think I was a hooker, of course, which made things even sweeter for me.

There never seemed to be enough candles for me, and picking the right music was of the utmost importance. I always had clean white sheets on all the furniture, and every piece of equipment was laid out carefully on the table. I used to try to predict what would be used first and put the pieces in order according to my predictions. Typically, it started with a paddle and the last piece would be the cane.

As I've previously mentioned, I eventually gave up doing sessions altogether since I felt it was a conflict for me to session when I was the owner. I preferred the Ladies to do the sessions, and I was happy to go in for a guest appearance on occasion. I also enjoyed being wanted and denying myself to clients.

Once I had given up doing sessions, I felt that I could see Sir Robert outside the dungeon. I had known him for years now and had never broken the "no-fraternization" rule. I was not taking him away from other Ladies because I was the only one he saw now. It was time for our relationship to evolve.

# DATE WITH DESTINY

As you know, *The Story of O* was my favorite book. It was the first thing in my life I found that had affirmed to me that there were others like me out there! I modeled myself as a submissive after O, and in my mind, that was who I was. It was no surprise that I would be dressed in an O dress and cape with a chrome collar with chains connecting to matching cuffs for my first date with Sir Robert.

Where does one go dressed like this? There was a great place on Santa Monica Boulevard called the French Market that was one of my favorite places to eat. It was the best place ever, if only because of the beautiful array of people that frequented this West Hollywood restaurant. On any given day, you could go there and see old Ladies having lunch together, sitting at a table next to a couple of drag queens. It was beautiful. It was no surprise to anyone when we turned up for dinner, and I was dressed this way.

This was our first time out together, and I felt so beautiful because I was out and completely who I was. Sir Robert loved every minute of it, as I could tell by the pride on his face as we sat down at our table. It was perfection being somewhere safe in who I was. Dinner was served and we had our meal like it was just another day. I could feel people looking at me, not in a bad way but in more of a "welcome to the family" way. It was a beautiful meal, but I could not tell you what I had to eat.

When we finished, we went to The Pleasure Chest to do some shopping. I felt like a queen entering the store on my leash. We created quite a stir and people came and talked to Robert as I kept my head down and was silent unless given permission to speak. Walking through the store was just glorious. This was a long-time fantasy of mine coming true. We bought a couple of things, and then we left.

When I got in the car, Sir Robert put a blindfold on me. Things just kept getting better and better. I was now 100 percent in my O zone. We drove for some time, and I kept listening for sounds that might give away where we were, but never did figure it out. The longer I was in the car, the more my mind raced. I had never trusted anyone this much nor felt so free. I could feel the car turn into a driveway and slow down to park. Where was I? At another dungeon? Nothing felt familiar to me. It was very exciting.

The car stopped, and I sat in my seat. He came to my door and opened it. I was still blindfolded, and when I got out of the car, I felt very uneasy with every step I took, but he was an excellent guide. I could hear voices as I walked and decided to myself I was at The Chateau in Roissy on my way to the Enclave. There were stairs, and I was frightened but took comfort in hearing his voice guide me up the stairs. We reached the top, walked a few feet, and came to a door. I heard the turn of the key, and then I was led into a room. He did not speak, nor did I.

Another door was opened, and I was in a room with my hands cuffed together and my leash attached to something to limit my movement. I was left in the room for what seemed an eternity, and my mind went wild. Were there others there? I did not hear any more voices but imagined I was in some dark, cold room illuminated by candles and I was being watched. It is hard not to fidget after a while but I tried very hard to hold my place. The door opened, the leash was unhooked, and I was taken to another room. I knelt on the floor, and the magic began.

Wearing a blindfold for long periods of time intensifies everything, and our play was on another level. He was very good at getting into my head. I liked the feeling of being frightened but knowing I was safe. This would be the first night I would give myself totally to him in my "chateau in France" in The Enclave. When the blindfold finally came off, once my eyes adjusted to the dim light in the room, I could see where I was. I was in a motel, and it was perfect. BDSM is a mind trip and he excelled at psychological play. He was The Master. He was my Sir Robert, and I was definitely his submissive.

# FLIGHTS OF FANTASY

Since Sir Robert lived in England, our relationship was long-distance. Add in my fear of flying, and it wasn't the ideal situation – but we made it work. I had never been out of the country other than a high school trip to Stratford, Ontario, for a Shakespeare festival and a trip in and out of Tijuana once. When Sir Robert invited me to go to England for the first time, I was beside myself. I did not have a passport, of course, so that had to be dealt with, but once I got it, I was officially a traveling sub.

I found myself a travel doctor to give me the drugs that I needed to fly. I was lucky enough that Robert came over to get me before the first flight to Europe. This definitely made things easier for me, but I was still scared shitless. I tried to put myself in submissive mode for the flight, which did not work at all. He was very compassionate and patient with me and explained every noise the plane made to me. I tried to sleep, but that was not a possibility, even with the Ativan and Ambien I had taken. He got no sleep either because I was so much work.

Once we landed at Heathrow, I was not feeling well. My super sexy jet-setter lifestyle was not working out too well for me. Getting through customs took forever, and all I wanted to do was get out of the airport and get home! We went to his car, and I got in his pride-and-joy Jaguar XK8. It was perfect for traveling down the winding

country lanes we would use to get to his house. It did not take long for me to get car sick, and he had to pull off to the side of the road to experience the joy of me vomiting out of his car door. Better out than in, I guess, but very humiliating. It is one of those things we still laugh about. It took me about three days to get over the jet lag. I am a horrible traveler, which sucks because I love it so much!

He was renting a house as he had left his home with his ex when he left, and the house was fitted out with antique furniture and a cozy couch that looked out the backyard. I loved sitting on the couch once I learned I could see all four seasons of the year happen in one day in England.

After a while, he found an adorable little annex at an old schoolhouse out in the country. It was small and cozy, and it was ours. I made it our home, and he called it "The Bunny Hutch," which was perfect for many reasons… for my name and for the hundreds of bunnies that congregated in the yard every day. It was perfection. It was like living in a Beatrix Potter house. The added bonus was that it was close to the best fish-and-chips shop of all time!

One of my favorite memories is coming down the country lane in the middle of the night in the rain, and our song "Angel" came on the radio. He stopped the car, came around to my side, opened the door, and gave me his hand. We danced in the rain that night, and I will always cherish this memory. It was the most romantic moment of my life up until that moment.

My first trip to London just blew my mind. I am a British history freak, and to be able to walk through the streets of London and just soak up all the history, there was more than I had ever imagined I would be able to do in my lifetime. I felt like a princess the entire time I was with him. I was living a life I never dreamed possible, and I loved it. I loved it when he went to work, and I waited for his return. I loved making him dinner and cleaning the house using the strange little vacuum cleaner and the different household cleaners. Everything was a precious moment to me. I loved the experience of just being the little woman. I had always worked during my marriages and while being a single mother, so I did not get much opportunity to experience the joy of being a homemaker. This tickled my domestic fancy very much.

There were so many cool fetish clubs and shops to experience that it would take more than one trip to enjoy them all. I knew I would take on this lifestyle very quickly. I had led a very simple life and never had opportunities to experience real elegance and fine debauchery! There was a lot to learn. One thing I learned, and I was very self-conscious of, was that I talked loudly. I only discovered this because all the women I met were so soft-spoken, and when I opened my mouth, I felt like a loud, drunk uncle during the holidays.

# KINKY PRETTY WOMAN

The first time we went shopping for some fetish clothes in

England, I was blown away because there were so many places to go and not enough time! House of Harlot was the first place he took me, and he bought me a beautiful electric blue latex gown, which has managed to survive the test of time, and I still have it. I became a very good customer and returned many times on future trips. Camden Market was a great place to go for fetish wear as well, and this was like Disneyland to me. There was Murray and Vern and Fairy Godmother and Cobbler to The World, not to mention smaller little shops inside the Camden marketplace. Inner Sanctum, Honour, and Skin Two were in different parts of town, and over the years, they would all know us and were always happy to see us.

Robert is a great negotiator, and being able to buy gifts for the Ladies who worked with me was a joy. Christmas was special when I was traveling because I was able to buy amazing outfits for the Ladies during my trips. Watching the faces of the Ladies opening up their gifts was a real feel-good moment for me. Most of them had never owned a leather or latex piece, and cinching submissives into their first real corsets was loads of fun. It was a real blessing for me to be able to do this for them at first.

But the problem that eventually came into play was that they did not want to wear them to work, because they thought the outfits were too nice to work in. So they wore them to the clubs instead. Some missed the plot, which was to look fabulous at work, take pictures, and make more money. Eventually, this became a big

source of frustration for me, so those shopping sprees came to a halt. I never regretted doing it because it made me so happy, but it became pretty pointless in the end.

I went back and forth to Britain for years and had so many amazing BDSM experiences. Let's face it: the Europeans know how to do it! Torture Garden is one of the most popular BDSM events worldwide. I attended my first Torture Garden party in an old Church in Brixton. Everyone was dressed to the nines. You could smell the latex when you entered the building. There were several floors and several rooms with different music playing in each of them, and the floors shook with all the people dancing and the thump of the music. It was intoxicating. Hands down, the Europeans have the best fetish events. I think they have better access to quality fetish clothing in Europe, and there is so much custom work done for these events that it feels like all things are possible.

For years, when I was traveling on a regular basis, I got such a thrill of being able to purchase beautiful corsets from Axfords of London and adorable PVC and latex outfits from Honour. I was lucky enough to go to Demask in Amsterdam and purchase a beautiful black latex cape with red stripes and a fantastic military coat that just screamed fantasy! These are still part of the treasures I cherish to this day.

The Sex Maniacs' Ball was an event not to be forgotten. It was a huge event on a pier and hedonism at its finest. You never knew

what you were going to walk into from room to room. You could have just gotten a snack, and then walked into an orgy, and continued to a room full of kinksters with Dominant men vying for the title of "Best Air Flogger." I always found it interesting when I attended kink events that so many of the Dominant men were into the performance aspect of the play but that they paid very little attention to the submissives themselves.

The men loved watching themselves in the mirror as they flogged someone so much that they could hardly take their eyes off themselves! Most had been diligently practicing the ever-popular "Florentine flogging" technique, which is basically using two of the same type of floggers and then flogging in a figure-eight motion. It was lovely to watch, but I always preferred seeing the connection between players who were truly connected. It made such an obvious difference, and it was a beautiful thing to witness.

There were smaller events at pubs as well as the big parties, and again, everyone dressed to impress. The first time I saw a penis nailed to a board was at one such party. *Yes, you read that right.* I was in awe of the seriousness of the play going on at these parties. I went to a Corset Ball where we all had dinner together with chamber music playing and then partied after dinner in another room. There just never seemed to be an end to the events that went on in London, and I longed for it so much every time I returned home.

We went to Hamburg, where we visited underground and

claustrophobic dungeons. I had always heard that in Germany, the play was intense, so while there, we engaged the services of "Extreme Slavkin Helga." Sir was going to play with both of us, but we weren't in the room ten minutes before she was trying to get Sir Robert to fuck her. I stayed in my role, which was extremely difficult because I wanted to take the flogger and extremely flog her! I was so taken aback. But of course, I had to remember I was in another country and remind myself what the ramifications of an arrest would be for me. Sir put her in her place and denied her the privilege. Sir knew me so well. He just knew I would want to show up this cheeky bitch, so of course, he showed her what extreme play was with me. I must admit, I have always been very competitive and was always up to shock people with how much pain I was willing to take.

We were at a party in Amsterdam in a huge space that had a large room and several smaller rooms in it. There were quite a few people there, but not a lot going on. Sir Robert decided to cane me, which brought in an audience to the big room. He gave me 100 strokes of the cane, and I could hear the 'ooooohs' and 'aaahhhhs' of the people in the audience. I felt so beautiful and amazing to elicit awe from those watching, so of course, when he finished with the 100 strokes, I had to get sassy with him and challenge him, which I knew would get me more. He threatened to give me another 100, and I replied with a "whatever"-type of remark, and it was on.

Some of the viewers were begging him not to do it. It was too

much. Not for Bunny! It was game on! I counted every stroke out loud and reveled in the lament of some of the audience members. After the last stroke hit, Sir pulled me up from the horse, and I could feel how proud he was of me in his hug. People clapped and congratulated us as we left.

This happened at a spanking party we attended in Birmingham, England. We had gone to the Moonglow Spanking Party, and I've got to tell you, it was one of the most British events I had ever attended up to that point. It took place in a large apartment, and I believe the Ladies who were there were being paid to be there. There were about 20 folding chairs arranged in a semi-circle in the middle of the room, and when the time came to play, they were filled with all these men sitting up very straight and looking very proper.

The way this worked was one Lady would go around the room, and each gentleman would give her a specified number of swats with the hand. Then she would get up, he would say, "Thank you very much," and she moved to the next until she had done the entire circle. Then, another Lady repeated the cycle until they had all been spanked. It was like they were having tea or something, all proper and adorable... but it was so hard for me not to laugh. They were hardly even getting hit! I don't think anyone wanted to appear too mean in front of the other men or something. I kept trying to imagine this scenario back home and just could not picture it.

Then, it was time for a break and refreshments. This afforded

Sir Robert and I the opportunity to play by ourselves, and, of course, the cane was the implement of choice. He knew I would want it hard, so he accommodated me. We definitely kicked things up a notch, and the Moonglow Spanking Club was never the same again after we left!

I loved my British life. It was the ultimate escape from reality for me and my childhood dream had come to fruition. I loved being dressed in my latex maid's outfit on my knees with a cane in my mouth at the front door when my Master came home. It was the best life. I was a completely different person and was the happiest I had ever been.

Robert was a dream. My history made me feel very insecure, worthless, and sometimes just downright ugly. But with him, I always felt beautiful. It's hard to explain, but it was difficult for me to trust my happiness, and I could never get what he saw in me that was so damned wonderful. I could see how much he loved me but could never figure out why. I know it bothered him, and to this day, self-deprecation is still my specialty. Accepting a compliment is almost painful at times because I just cannot believe it is sincere.

I have never doubted how much Robert loves me because I come with a lot of baggage. I will never forget the pain on his face when he reached over to put his arm around me, and I flinched in fear. It was a reflex, and I had no control over it, but I could see it affected him deeply. We had a long talk about it and when we were

done, he understood it had nothing to do with him. I am loved, and I know it to be true.

# CALIFORNIA DREAMIN'

Flash forward to 2001. Sir Robert and I had just bought a home together the year prior, even though he was still living in England and I was over here in the U.S. I took care of the remodeling and getting the house in shape for us to both enjoy together one day, I hoped. His business was keeping him away for longer periods of time, so every occasion was much more special.

My birthday was in November, and I was expecting him to come. As the day got closer, he said that he would not be able to come because his business would not allow him to escape this year. I was devastated, but I did not believe him at the same time. He always said, "Expect the unexpected," so I did. I prepared everything and myself like he was going to show up, and he was just messing with me. He engaged with some of my friends to get them to take me out so I would not be too miserable on my day.

On my birthday, my friends and I were going to meet at The Mustache Café on Melrose. I still expected him to show up. Everywhere I went the entire day, I felt I would see him around the corner.

When I came home, I ran up my stairs to the bedroom, expecting him to be there. There were "Happy Birthday" and "I'm sorry I could not be there" signs from him on the routes I traveled, on stop signs, and on telephone poles made by my friends. I spent

the entire day anticipating him showing up somewhere. It was such an emotional roller coaster!

Expectations up, then the letdown. I was a wreck. It was time to go to the restaurant and meet my wonderful friends. When I arrived, everyone was already there at a table. I got all my hugs and condolences that Robert could not come, but we would still have a great time. We were yacking as one does with a group of friends, and a huge bouquet of long-stemmed red roses appeared with one of the waiters. I took the flowers and found the card with wishes for a happy birthday and that He could be there. I burst into tears because this made it real for me. He was not coming. I was bummed. The waiter came around to get our drink order. I loved piña coladas, but now I was in a mood and just wanted a Diet Coke.

A little while later, it seemed as if every waiter in the joint was around our table, and I was praying it was not the "Happy Birthday" song. I was not in the mood. The drinks came to the table. I was sitting facing the wall, so when a piña colada was put in front of me, I turned around to the waiter to tell him I did not order a piña colada! The waiter was standing there with a towel over his arm, and I could feel everyone waiting for something. It took time for it to register in my mind, and when it did, the entire restaurant began clapping. It was Sir Robert. He had done it again! An entire 24-hour mind fuck, and I loved him all the more for it. I did get in trouble for being rude to the waiter, though!

While Los Angeles kink was a far cry from European fun and games, we did manage to find things to do to amuse ourselves. I really enjoyed going to parties and events, and when I went with him, I was Bunny. I always felt people were happy to see us and knew there would be some good play if we were there. There were not a lot of places to go, but we found a home at Lair de Sade, which was a great play space run by another kinky couple.

The first time we went to the Lair, it was held at Nob Hill, a hall of sorts in the Valley with two floors and several rooms. There were vendors on the first floor. This was the first time I discovered The Stockroom, a BDSM store. They did not have a storefront at the time and sold at events put on by local kinksters. I was always up for buying good equipment for the business, and I got some good deals. There were others, but The Stockroom was my go-to at the time.

The second floor was where the play took place. I was wearing my custom-made O dress with six-inch stilettos, which made navigating the carpeted floors a little difficult at times. One of the great things about Sir Robert was his creative play… the kind you do without having to lift a finger or break a sweat but just fuck with someone's head. We played some upstairs, and I was blindfolded.

After we played, he left the blindfold on me and walked me around a bit. Then he parked me against a wall and told me to wait, which, of course, I did. Time always seems to stand still when you are blindfolded. You become a little high when in submissive mode

and "unaware." I was very proud of who I was and how beautiful I felt. Sir Robert returned to me and told me to follow him. I waited for the blindfold to be removed but that was not happening. He was going down the stairs and wanted me to follow him blindfolded. I was terrified. He just kept saying, "Follow the sound of my voice." I managed to grab the railing, but I felt like I was standing at the edge of a cliff and would fall, and my legs were shaking.

I could hear him calling my name, and I took a step without knowing how deep the step was. Every step was torture. I could feel everyone watching me, so I did not want to muck it up. I don't remember at what point I decided to sit on my ass and go down. I was hysterical by now and jumping at every sound. I was the star of the show, and I had gone from beautiful, graceful submissive to clown on her butt sliding down the stairs. When I made it to the bottom, Sir Robert was right there and helped me up and hugged me. He was so proud of me. Everyone was clapping. I was happy to suffer for my public. It was great. We made our mark!

The next time we went, they had acquired a huge space in North Hollywood with lots of rooms and interesting equipment. It had the atmosphere of a backyard barbecue because we all knew each other, and there was always food in the kitchen. It was great to hang out and chat and play with like-minded people who accepted who we were. I was Lady Hillary by now, which created a bit of conflict for me at some of these events. I loved Bunny. Bunny was my strength

and the special part of me that was a badass, even as a submissive. I knew exactly who I was, and I reveled in every moment of Bunny.

Sadly, as time went on, being Lady Hillary was a conflict for me at the parties. We had started bringing some of the Ladies to the parties to play and meet potential clients, which made it hard to be Bunny on those nights, and Lady Hillary was keeping an eye on the Ladies. People wanted us to become the Domme couple, which I was not into in any way, shape, or form. We continued to go, but my role was changing. I found myself looking after lost subbies and making sure they were okay all night, which put a damper on my enjoyment, so I lost interest in going.

The last time I went was on Robert's 55th birthday. I had planned a great night and invited our friends and any of the Ladies who wished to attend. I wore my latex maid's outfit, which was his favorite. The cake was epic: It was me in my maid's outfit in the downward dog pose, and my ass was in the air with cane strikes on it. It was the best. It was a great night of play and camaraderie. Later in the evening, I gathered up some of my closest friends to witness my surprise gift to my Sir. We found an empty room and claimed it. I laid out the equipment I brought for this part of the evening. Understand that on this night, it had been quite some time since I was submissive in a public setting. I asked one of my friends to find Robert, and I positioned myself on the floor, kneeling in the present position while I anticipated his arrival.

In my hands was a Lochgelly Tawse school belt for my offering. The tawse was the weapon of choice for disciplining errant Scottish children. It is a belt about 2 feet in length, split in two about halfway down the tawse. It is a very intense piece of equipment, and I am glad I only knew it in a consensual situation. The tawse was a very special part of our play, as we used to start each session by tawsing my hands. As I got older, it became harder to do due to some physical limitations, so we had to shelve this precious part of our ritual. The room was silent. Not everyone knew what was going to happen.

In honor of his birthday, I was going to offer myself to him for a caning. When he entered the room, my head was down, and my eyes were on the floor, as they always were in our play. I could hear the surprise and pleasure in his voice as he entered. He bent down to kiss me and asked about the tawse. He did not feel good about doing it. I begged him to tawse my hands. I wanted to give that gift of my devotion to him tonight. He accepted and it was to be six on each hand as before. I could tell he was emotional about it. It was a grand gesture of my love to him, and he felt it.

My Sir took the tawse from my hands and I kept my hands palms up to receive his pleasure. He did not hold back as he knew it would hurt my heart for him to do so. This was so important and so beautiful for both of us. The guests in the room became emotional because they could feel us. The sound of the tawse hitting my palms

reverberated in the room, as did the stifled moans from my lips after every strike. It was so special and so beautiful, and I felt so lucky to have such a man love me. When he had finished with the tawse, he kissed the palms of my hand tenderly.

He was totally up for the caning. I always enjoyed taking a cane in public because I liked the gasps from the onlookers when I received nothing but the best strikes from my Sir. I love the swish sound of the cane as it finds its mark. It was so intense, and I was able to once again prove my submissive badassery to a small group of people who deserved the honor. This was a sweet and blissful moment and a memory I can cherish forever. Best birthday present ever!

There was a nightclub on Santa Monica Boulevard called Peanuts that, one night a week, became Sin-a-Matic, where the kinksters would go to dance and meet like-minded people. There was a small playroom in the back of the club where you could watch a scene. It was usually pre-ordained who would be playing, and as a rule, whoever it was, had great skills and we learned a lot watching this. It was nice to have a place where we could dance and drink and let loose. You never knew who you would run into when you went, and that was part of the fun.

There was also a stage in the main room where there was always a variety of kinky dancers or short little scenes happening. There was never a shortage of people who wanted to be in those spots. I

really enjoyed going to Sin-a-Matic, and afterward, we could walk next door to the French Market for a bite to eat and chill before going home. As I mentioned before, the French Market was one of my favorite places. On any given day, you could have a great meal and dine with an amazing group of people. It was like we imagined America should be. The mix was gay/lesbian, little old ladies who lunched, drag queens, straight locals, and kinksters. No judgment, just everyone united in the common bond of wanting some lunch! I loved it there. I tried to go back some years later to find it gone and it broke my heart. So many beautiful memories were made there, including lots of lunches with Lady Laura.

One event that I had been looking forward to was the Masque. It was to be an Eyes Wide Shut atmosphere with dinner and play. It was somewhere downtown. I was, of course, dressed to perfection with the most beautiful Venetian mask that I had gotten in Venice on my last trip. Who knew it would come in handy one day? The event was a little chaotic at times, but a good effort until a buzz began in the room that we needed to get out because there was going to be a raid. Evidently, there was quite a bit of cocaine floating around the playrooms, and that was a recipe for disaster. It was a shame because it did have so much potential.

I must honestly say that it always amazed me how lame events could be in LA. Basically, in this country at the time, it was New York and LA where things were happening in the kink world. I

always felt that wardrobe was a huge part of the scene. We had so many places to buy gear: Dream Dresser, Syren Latex, Trashy Lingerie, and Playmates on Hollywood Boulevard, along with a multitude of shoe shops specializing in fetish footwear. I never understood why people did not put in the effort when going out or even working. It always blew my mind that they could not grasp the importance of the fetish gear to the clients.

I applauded legendary party promoter Robert Fluty when he came to town and gave us the Kinkball, because the dress code was enforced. Robert was from New York and had his own club in the city for a while before relocating to Los Angeles. I used to have trouble dealing with the Bondage Ball because anyone could come in, and some real creeps would just stroll in off the streets and act like idiots. They were, of course, in T-shirts and jeans, and when they discovered submissive women in the building, they felt like they had hit the jackpot and could just assault them at will. There was more than one occasion a submissive had to be rescued from these morons. I did not go to many… perhaps I was a snob, or maybe I just felt that kink was due more respect and that the Ladies should be revered and not subjugated by a bunch of thrill seekers. This may have changed since I last attended one, so I cannot speak on it now.

The Kinkball was awesome. The Ladies all dressed to the nines, and we rented a limo that night and arrived in style. We were in a VIP section, and the Ladies performed magnificently throughout the night. There is nothing like the feeling of walking into a fetish event

where the music is thumping, and the smell of rubber overwhelms you when you walk in the door. Everyone is so beautiful, enjoying the freedom of being their kinky selves with no judgment or persecution. There were scantily clad Ladies dangling from hoops hanging from the ceiling. You could hear the gasps from bystanders, watching two men pull themselves up to the eaves by the hooks in their backs and nipples. It was like standing in the middle of Dreamland, just trying to absorb all the wonderful things happening.

Afterward, it was great fun going through town in the limo with the sunroof open, spanking Ladies while they were enjoying the wind rushing through their hair as they hung out of the top of the limo. To cap off the evening, a trip to McDonald's was always in order just for the pure pleasure of exhibitionism!

I must admit I was a bit of an exhibitionist. I loved freaking people out, whether it be from getting my ass caned 500 times or strutting alone through a Las Vegas casino dressed in a blue latex gown. I could feel all eyes on me as I made my way through the vast reception area and received many offers of an escort to get me to my car. There is nothing better than making an entrance at a fetish event incognito. I attended a Shadowlane event in Palm Springs and came dressed in a latex catsuit and hood with a long black ponytail with a mask on my face.

Although it was a spanking event, I could have spent most of the evening with someone across my latex lap spanking them, and

they would have been blissful. This is one of the great things about BDSM: becoming someone other than your real self. I built my own little fantasy world and lived in it quite happily for over forty years. I was a badass submissive who became a badass Domina over time. Living in this alternate universe to my reality helped me so much mentally and financially, as it did for many other women who have passed through this world over the years.

# MOM IS A DOMINATRIX

While I had created my own little bubble where things went my way and my fantasies were reality, there was always the dark cloud of "the real world" hanging over my head when I had to leave the safety and warmth of my dungeon world.

Being a single mom and a sex worker is not the ideal resume for the real world. I was always hiding something, and, being a fairly honest person, I am not a great "storyteller." I could not tell anyone what my job was and had to constantly make up things to adapt to my current situation.

Sex work is a real job. We pay our taxes, and we are responsible human beings. It did not matter whether you had sex or not; you were branded a "sex worker" if you had anything to do with adult entertainment.

In the sex industry that I worked in, we did not have sex with our clients. The most important part of BDSM is getting into someone's head. That is where it all begins. You can terrify someone without ever touching them if you know what you are doing. Making someone believe something is going to happen to them is the best part of the game.

Nevertheless, I could not get an apartment without lying about my job and always lived in constant fear that I would be found out.

When you have children, it is especially difficult to navigate the school years and all that goes with being a mom. You must develop your bullshit techniques and keep your stories straight. Back in the day, so many women who were working to take care of their children had to fight to keep them if a jealous boyfriend or ex-husband was in the picture because that is the first thing they would go for if you fell out with them. Women were reported to CPS, and men would send law enforcement to the place you worked, so you were pretty much held hostage to do their bidding. Many Ladies, including myself, had to pay off these men to get them out of their lives, and there was no guarantee they would not return for more.

The hardest thing was keeping it from your children. I don't even remember what I told my kids I did for work. I think I told them I was an office manager. They knew the building I worked in but never understood why they could not go in it. I had a million excuses. They all knew Lady Laura and adored her. They called her "Other Mother." They knew I worked for her, and when asked, she would just tell them "import/export," which was good because no one had a clue what that meant.

I always had a bit of an edge to me because of the way I dressed, and they just thought I was a cool mom. I was very careful to protect my children from my big secret for so many reasons, including that I did not want them to think I was a hooker. That is always the first image people would have if you said that you worked in a dungeon. The few times I did tell someone what I really did for a living, I

would find myself quickly blurting out the no-sex disclaimer. I have no problem with prostitution. The fact is that if I had not found BDSM, I would not have been able to support my children and provide them with some of the nice things kids need or want, like food, clothing, and shoes when they were growing up. I never wanted my children to be ashamed of me, and that was my deepest fear when they were growing up.

I came home from work one day to find a copy of the adult newspaper *LA Express* (where I advertised) spread out on my living room floor, and my first thought was, "OH, SHIT! My boys had it." I did not make a big deal of it but just picked it up and put it out of reach, and nothing was said. It did let me know that, eventually, I was going to have to tell my children. They were in high school and probably could take it by now. MTV helped me so much with this because I could make it relatable to rock-and-roll!

I told all my children when they turned 16. It was always the same: *"I know you probably wonder sometimes why my job keeps me away so much and what exactly do I do."* I always told them I was a Dominatrix, which at the time was stretching the truth a bit. Being a Dominatrix was considered cool – with the clothes, plus the fact you get to "beat up men." *"That is so cool, Mom!"* With my daughter, I answered some questions, then warned her: *"Don't tell your brothers – they aren't ready yet."* I could never tell them I was submissive… especially my sons, who were super protective of me.

(Good boys! ) There is no way that would sit in their minds well. I am certain they never knew about my submissive side until my relationship with my current husband. When I think about it today, every one of my kids had the same response. They told me they loved me and did not care what I did. I was their mom. It still makes me teary-eyed when I think about it.

I really tried to keep them as removed from my work situation as possible. As my daughter got older, I knew I did not want her to ever do what I did for a living. I was not keen on Ladies fresh out of high school doing this for their first job. I always felt I had some weird advantage because I was older when I started, I was certain about my sexuality, and I already had a pretty good read on the male species. I felt it was better for them to know themselves better before trying this. Of course, there are always exceptions to the rule. Some young women who came to me at 18 had been involved in BDSM for a couple of years!

I was certain that coming in at a young age would skew a girl's perception of men, and I did not want that. I eventually changed my hiring minimum age to 21 because of this. Yes, they made a lot of money when they were fresh off the farm. Clients loved seeing them because they were so young and naïve; they thought they could get away with more, which sometimes was the case in spite of any training we tried to give. I needed them to be safe. My decision was a good one. My daughter went to school of her own volition and worked her way up the corporate ladder in her field to be a badass

Lady Boss like her mom. She is much smarter than I am, and I am very proud of her.

My kids were awesome, but my absence sometimes gave them too much free time, which created a few problems. I struggled like most single moms with the guilt of not being home when my kids came home from school, not having enough money to get them everything they wanted, and not having money to send them through college or buy them the latest fashions. They all had their struggles, but I did the best I could, as any mom would. They could always make me laugh even when they made me angry, like the time my sons took all my Tupperware to use for paintball targets or when they were riding their bikes around the pool and even into it. I had to put the kibosh on them riding off the roof into the pool, which probably could have killed them!

We had a good relationship overall, and for all the shit we went through together, they have all grown up to be amazing people. *Yeah, I did that!*

I always said I would have sold my ass on a corner to take care of my kids, and I meant it sincerely. They were my world, and I wanted the best for them. I still do.

# THE TIMES, THEY ARE CHANGIN'

Everything changes, this I know. The stigma of BDSM was changing slowly, with the likes of Madonna helping us along. She was a huge influence in taking us out of the closet. Was that a good thing? There are pros and cons to everything, and this was no exception. I'll start with the good things. It gave people permission to give BDSM a try. People wanted to learn about BDSM and sought out our services to educate themselves. It was great for business.

However, there were lots of negatives. Many people, in general, now thought BDSM looked easy and that anyone could do it. Abusive types thought seeing a submissive gave them a license to beat women up. I used to cringe anytime I heard the words "beat up" in an interview. We tried to educate them, but these types thought they knew it all and they were "paying for us," which gave them the right to treat us like shit! My hard limits became, *"You cannot spit on me. I am not going to bark or oink like a pig, and if I say mercy, that means stop!"* Don't get me wrong… there were some very kind clients, but there was a whole new breed coming in now.

What made it worse? The Internet! The horrible abusive porn on the Internet raised the expectations of what a submissive would do in a session for some. The Internet was great for raising

awareness that we were here and ready to play, but the overall cost, in my opinion, at that time, was just not worth it.

Advertising changed. The audience you could reach on the Internet was incredible, but there were unscrupulous people advertising on sites like Backpage.com, which most people in the industry felt was a platform for prostitution. The ads were blatant and shocking, with Ladies advertising that they were young and would do drugs with you. "Anything goes" was pretty much the message. When it first started, a lot of people in the scene began using it because it was so cheap, and you could pay by the day. It was bad, and I was so glad when they shut it down. The world became a little safer that day!

I loved my secret little closed-off fantasy world, where no one should be allowed in unless they were sincere and knew what they were doing. I was "Old School," and this was not a hobby for me. It was my passion, and I needed it for my mental well-being.

The more people that heard about BDSM and that they could go somewhere and practice it, the quicker things changed. Suddenly, it was a lucrative job for a woman who may have been beautiful but was clueless about the lifestyle. Club owners were thrilled with the extra flow of cash coming in, but the Ladies who had been around a while with the actual skills were being overlooked and began to lose money to these newbie know-nothings who, most of the time had little regard for the house rules and caused *"income interruptus"* for

the other Ladies. You could not say anything to the boss because then you were seen as jealous or petty, and if they were bringing in the cash, no one really cared. It was a damn shame. I tried very hard to ensure that the Ladies who worked with us, who didn't have the skills, at least had the desire to learn.

When I first took over The Dominion, I interviewed all of the Ladies who came through and made the hiring decisions myself. I would hire someone if I had a soft spot for them, and they seemed eager. I am not saying I wasn't good at it, but anyone who knows me knows I have high anxiety, and sometimes, I tend to get off topic or talk in circles. At one point in time, I made myself an outline to follow, but I was miserable at it. I was never afraid of admitting to my weaknesses, which I actually think is a strength. So when Lady Francesca joined me, hiring the Ladies became solely her job, and she was great at it. She's a great inquisitor and knew the Ladies' entire life stories by the end of the interview. She also made sure they were tested by senior staff before the official hire.

With the advent of the Internet, there were more clubs opening, plus lots of play parties going on throughout the city, and I grew concerned about the safety of play that was happening around town. People would go to the parties, see a flogger, and just start flailing it on someone with no clue as to where it should be landing. There are so many different types of equipment, and if used improperly, it could cause serious damage to someone.

I'll admit that I enjoyed going to some of the parties. It was a great time to be Bunny (my submissive self) and enjoy time with my Sir. I loved the feeling of walking into a party and being wanted. I was a legend, and not just in my own mind. I had a reputation as a heavy player, I always dressed impeccably, and I knew my place as a submissive and the protocol that went with it. I was in my element and loved every second of it. But things started to get complicated for me in these situations because I was a professional player, and when I saw things that were wrong, I really struggled to keep my mouth shut.

I felt I had a responsibility to tell a Dom who was caning a girl of 90 pounds full force on her back that was not a good idea. I was not easily dismissed even as a submissive, as I had already deemed myself a Diva submissive. Some of my clients went to these parties, and if I saw them being stupid that night, I had to let them know. Cleanliness is so hugely important at a play party.

One night, a naked man laid over a spanking horse and took a spanking, then when he was done, he just got up and walked away. I was on the other side of the room and yelled at him to clean up his mess. That wasn't going to happen on my watch! I marched over to get him and showed him where the disinfectant was. Once he had cleaned it to my satisfaction, I let him go and returned to my sweet subby self with my Sir...

We had some dear friends we would meet at the parties,

including some real Old-School superstars like Lord Dan Sir (God rest his soul), who was a legendary edge player. Edge play can involve playing with fire, knives, piercing, asphyxiation, and beyond. Edge play is serious stuff, and you must know and trust your partner to participate in this type of play. Lord Dan Sir was a bondage Master and liked mummification. One night, he had his beautiful partner completely wrapped, including her head in Saran wrap, on a large bondage table. He always drew an audience, and I went in with my Sir to see what all the buzz was about. When I saw her completely wrapped up like that, my claustrophobic self about lost it, but it was so beautiful to witness that I could not look away.

He had a knife in his hand and was talking to her. They had practiced this so many times to make sure she would be safe. I really admired her bravery and the gift of this trust she was able to give her Master. I don't know how long she was in this situation because my brain was fried, but I felt so much relief when he took the knife and cut the mouth open on the wrap. He unwrapped her slowly and had blankets ready for her because she was going to be cold when the wrap came off. The tenderness in the aftercare between a true Master and his submissive is so beautiful to witness. I felt so honored to have been able to witness this moment. But would I ever do it? Hell no!

I used to encourage the staff to attend some of these parties because there were a lot of single men who attended, and one could meet new clients in this situation. As more of the staff attended, it

became very difficult for me to be my submissive self at these parties. I was becoming Lady Hillary, who brought beautiful, submissive women to the party. I was not being viewed as the submissive I wanted to be. There would be people looking for a Domme couple to play with, and that was just not my scene. A lot of the Ladies wanted to play with my Sir and I understood that because he was trustworthy and knew what he was doing, but it was difficult.

I honestly have to say, I resented it when I had to transition from sub to Switch or Domme. Being submissive was my happy place and where I drew my strength from. Sometimes, I wish I had run the club as a submissive and not Lady Hillary. Submissives are brilliant people who have just as much business savvy as any Dominant. I thought about it a lot over the years but just kept it to myself. I am certain my submissive side is the side that made the business thrive. I was honest and not afraid to get my hands dirty to keep the place clean. (My OCD helped with this enormously.) I wanted everyone to have a wonderful experience when they came in, and did my best to ensure this would be the case.

On the other hand, my submissive side made cupcakes and had them on the desk, which cracked people up when they came in. I did not want people to feel too nervous when they first arrived, so I made the environment as non-threatening as possible. Countless people commented on how friendly The Dominion was and how

comfortable they felt once they got inside the doors. The expectation was that we would all be a bunch of surly bitches treating men badly as soon as they walked in. I would joke with them and tell them that it doesn't happen until you have paid for your session!

# INQUIRING MINDS WANT TO KNOW

There were many business opportunities I turned down while running The Dominion, and I never had a single regret about that. I mentioned earlier that I turned down countless reality TV offers because they seemed to me like a quick way to put yourself out of business. But those weren't the only offers I shot down. There was a period when every trash TV show was having Dominatrixes on, and I have to tell you, it rarely turned out well for the Domme. They were brought on to sensationalize, titillate, and eventually, in the end, be crucified publicly for what they did for a living.

Going on a mainstream talk show dressed in your gear with a man-dog on a leash next to you is not something people wanted to understand. The shows were not there to open people's minds, and no one in the audience was particularly interested in who they really were as human beings. I was invited, and thank God my anxiety always prevented me from doing things like this.

I also felt that a big part of our success was the discretion we practiced with our Ladies and our clients. We had times when the rag magazines would hang out in front of our place, and once, a news crew tried to get photos of the inside of the front door. All they got was a picture of a candle burning on an end table… big deal! We

had high-profile entertainers, public officials, and celebrities come through our doors, and never did anyone leak it to the press or anyone else. I was always proud of the Ladies for that because I knew they were offered big money for the stories. But their integrity was not for sale.

I was proud we survived all those years with no scandal.

# PANDEMIC

It was March of 2020, and like everyone else on the planet, we were trying to figure out what was going on and how to handle this mystery disease that was spreading like wildfire and killing people. No one was sure yet what was going on, and doctors and public officials were scrambling to try and figure out what the hell to do. I had to decide and do it quickly. Some of the Ladies were immediately freaked out and stopped working, and it was everyone's choice to do what they felt was best for their well-being. Some Ladies wanted to keep working because they had bills to pay, and getting unemployment as a sex worker was not a thing. I had a responsibility as Dungeon Mother to make sure my "kids" were safe, and I had to make the call that we would have to close up shop for a while until things were brought under control or figured out more.

On March 20, 2020, we closed the doors and stepped into a complete unknown, just like everyone else on the planet. I don't think anyone knew yet how devastating COVID-19 would be, and the world would never be the same again. We kind of felt like, *"Give it a few weeks, and we should be cool."* The uncertainty of it all was terrifying, not only because of the health risks of working but of the economic hardships that befell so many. It was such a sad and sobering day, the day we closed the doors to COVID-19.

Once we closed, I went to work several times a week just to take care of the building and to disinfect the crap out of the whole place. It gave me a purpose and kept me busy. It was gut-wrenching to walk into the lifeless building and be alone with her. We spent many hours sharing our pain while I was scrubbing her down and sterilizing her.

Days turned to weeks and then to months. One day, I had an idea that I could rent out the rooms to couples who perhaps had no place to play, and it would be a great diversion from what was going on in the world. I put a notice on the website that while we were closed, we would be open to room rentals. Well, this was a great idea. Couples began coming in slowly to play. It was a no-contact situation, and I did not rent out to more than one couple at a time, so they would have the entire building to themselves, which was a huge treat for them. Some began coming in every week. I would just let them in the building and leave an envelope on the desk in the lobby for the rental and when they were finished and left the building, I went over and cleaned up.

Everything was super disinfected, and I always cleaned the equipment they used as well. It made me so happy to see this because I felt it was a great outlet for them, and I know they appreciated it. Soon, a few of the Ladies asked to rent rooms, which I allowed with the same rules that I had for the couples. Eventually, I gave the Ladies keys so they could enter the building and do sessions when I would not be there. It worked out so well for

everyone.

The Dominion reopened on June 17, 2021. By this time, a lot of staff had moved on to other ventures, or some had moved back to their home states. I think most of us were a little afraid, but that made us smart about what we did. We required masking and proof of vaccination for anyone to come in. Before COVID, I had about 50 women working with me, and we were open seven days a week with a day shift and a night shift. Upon re-opening, I was only able to do two shifts a week with three to four Ladies on a day shift. This was fine, and I expected it to be that way at first. There was plenty of business to be had when we opened, but not enough staff to accommodate everyone's needs.

Lady Francesca was not ready to come back yet, so I did the desk on the two days we were open. In my mind, I felt eventually things would go back to normal, or we would adjust to the new normal. Lady Francesca came back in August, which was very helpful. I was still allowing special appointments during off-hours so the Ladies who did rentals when we were closed would still be able to continue with their clients. I could not get new Ladies into work because I wanted to honor the Ladies' wishes who were working. We just kept things to the "family" for the time being. I did hire one more person in August, and that was the extent of it. There were about four Ladies who kept the place going for a while.

We continued this way for some time, and eventually, I was

able to add one more day of shifts with the addition of a couple of Ladies added to the mix. But reliability was a big issue, so it was hard to be sure those committed to shifts would actually be there. I think one of my biggest disappointments was when the Ladies who I considered to be my friends and who had been with me for a long time did not show up. Sometimes, I felt like an ass for feeling hurt. Everyone had their own reasons, I guess. I am just not that person. I honor my commitments. But I just went with the flow and did the best I could.

Lady Francesca was stressed after the novelty of being back was gone. She had the patience of a saint and wanted everyone to succeed. Being at the desk and not having staff show up is very stressful.

I honestly thought we would be able to make it, and I suppose if I had wanted to run my business into the ground and go into debt doing so, I could have done that. I was also dealing with the passage of a new law in California, which went into effect in January of the year 2020. It was known as the "gig worker" bill, and it required companies that hired independent contractors to reclassify them as employees. I had always said if I had to make everyone employees, I would not be able to keep the business running. Many other small businesses felt the same.

We were looking into ways around it, but then COVID hit. *I can take a hint, Lord!* Not only were we dealing with that, but the

face of the neighborhood had been changing and we did not always feel the safest there at times. Venice Boulevard is a major street with a huge transient population, and we'd had some problems in this area, like people shitting on the sides of our buildings or passing out in the parking lot. There were some close calls in regard to our safety.

One night, a woman on something came banging on our door, wanting her kids back. She was so out of it, but she insisted that she knew her kids were upstairs in my building. (Spoiler alert: They weren't!) Poor Robert tried to handle it, but we did have to call the police. Before they arrived, she attacked Robert, and I had to pepper-spray her. It was a really sad situation, and after COVID, I did not really have much of a desire to run a night shift anymore for the safety of the staff. We did everything possible to get back on track, but there comes a point in time where you have to ask yourself, "Is it worth it?" In spite of the fact that most of the Ladies thought I went home and sat on my stacks of money at night, that just wasn't the case. While The Dominion was a very successful business, I put my money back into it to further its success. You have to be real with yourself. I was lucky that I owned the property my business was in.

I talked to Lady Francesca and, of course, my husband Robert on many occasions, trying to figure out what the best course of action would be. Francesca and I had made an agreement years ago

that we would be there for each other until the end. It was becoming a great stress for both of us. The decision had to be made, but it wasn't one I made lightly. I was getting on in years, and maybe if I had been 20 years younger, I would have stuck it out. Yet that was not to be. I had to make the heartbreaking decision to close the doors for good. I did not know what I would do without my Dominion. This was 42 years of my life, and I was in love with her. I never considered myself to be an astute businessperson, but I did possess a lot of common sense.

I was worried about everyone, but then, when I was real with myself, I figured out that not everyone was worried about me or The Dominion. I heard later that some Ladies felt I pulled the rug out from under them with the closure, which stung. I am sure they got over it. There were thousands of women who came through The Dominion over the years, and that was the thing. The Dominion was a step towards something better for most, and Ladies would come and go. It was not a career for most as it was for me. I was there, and the buck stopped with me. I was responsible for the safety of the staff and the success of the business. My business account was cleaned out during COVID. Bills still needed to be paid, and there was nothing coming in. We loaned the business money to reopen and prayed for the best.

If I had ever felt in my heart that The Dominion would be restored to her former glory, we would still be there. I could just see the writing on the wall. Sometimes, I had moments where I could

see my BDSM life flash before my eyes, and when this happened, I could be honest with myself and know that things had changed too much for me. BDSM was not what it was when I began. Ideas had changed about play and protocols, and respect had gone out the window. Francesca and I felt like dinosaurs. It was heartbreaking for us and frustrating as well.

Telling the Ladies was so difficult and emotional. There were a lot of tears for the few who were there with me. We had decided to put the buildings up for sale, and because the sale of commercial property at that time was not an easy task, we thought we would have six months to a year to shut things down and ease into the closure. Nothing was selling during COVID! We did explore options that may have been able to keep the doors open, but because we owned the property, it was impossible, and honestly, no one wanted the gig!

# CLOSURE - THE ANNOUNCEMENT

*Dear Dominion Friends and Family,*

*It is with great sorrow that I must announce the closure of The*

*Dominion in December.*

*The Dominion has been a legendary and magical place in the community since 1980, when Lady Laura first opened the doors of her West Hollywood apartment. It has been a safe place for kinksters to come and share their deepest, darkest fantasies without fear of judgment or reprisal. We have formed many wonderful relationships with our friends, and over the years, many legendary Dominas have learned their craft here and formed lifelong friendships with their kinky sisters.*

*I began my journey with Lady Laura in 1981. I was a true submissive, seeking a place to realize my dreams. Lady Laura's Dominion became the place for me! Lady Laura took me under her wing and made sure I was safe and remained sane in the process. Lady Laura was a true Diva whose boots I could never have filled. When she passed away in 1997, she left The Dominion in my care to carry on her legacy. I am proud of my years as a Dungeon Mother and the reputation of excellence The Dominion has attained all over the world. I took great pride in watching the Ladies grow from BDSM babies to blossom into some of the most amazing and experienced players in the business.*

*The Dominion was a sanctuary for those of us who were into BDSM. We learned from each other and supported each other because we loved BDSM and needed it. We took it very seriously. It was about OUR fantasies as much as our clients'. We loved what we*

*were doing. We learned from the bottom up in a safe and nurturing environment.*

*The heart and soul of commercial BDSM has changed dramatically, but mine hasn't. I find myself with the same high standards and Old-School values, unwilling to compromise them.*

*Since COVID-19, there have been many drastic changes to commercial BDSM, which makes it impossible to run The Dominion up to my standards. I cannot compromise my principles, so I must let Her go. I once asked Lady Laura how long I should keep it going, and she said, "Until it no longer brings you joy."*

*I tried my hardest to make this work after COVID, but The Dominion is more than just a room to rent. The Dominion is a place of sisterhood and pride in the work you do. It is the love and care for our friends who visit us every week or just when they can get into town. It is the happiness and pride you feel after doing a good session or the loving care you receive as a submissive if you had a bad session. It is a place of love and respect for each other and the Old-School values I had hoped to pass down to those receptive to the idea.*

*The Dominion has been my life for over 40 years. When I started, I was a meek submissive with no self-esteem. The love and care within these walls have made me a better and stronger person. I am proud of what I have done, and I wish I could continue, but it is not possible in this new era. I would rather shut it down with*

*dignity than compromise my values.*

*I started doing this over 40 years ago because I loved it, and I needed it. I am leaving it now because I love it too much to not honor the protocols, rituals, and honesty of those who mentored and raised me.*

*I thank all the Ladies who have passed through these doors for making The Dominion the legend it has become. I am so grateful to all our friends who visited us and played and trusted us with their fantasies.*

*You will never be forgotten.*

*I am sorry we must go, but please think of us fondly in the future,*

**All my kinky love and respect,**
**Lady Hillary.**

When the announcement was made, I was so touched by the outpouring of love from our clients. They were sad but grateful for what The Dominion had given them over the years. There were a lot of people who wanted to come in and do that last session with us, and the goodbyes were rough for me. I was delighted that some of the Ladies who I had worked with in years past, wanted to come in and play in one of the rooms one last time. It was lovely to see them again and be put back in touch, and I still see them to this day on occasion. I think the Old-School gang had a better appreciation and understanding of me, so talking to those who I could relate to again

was amazing.

Once we made the decision to sell, everything happened so quickly. We put the properties on the market on November 21, 2021, again thinking we would have all the time in the world, and we were very mistaken. The properties sold quickly, and everything was done and dusted in six weeks. We worked out a deal where we would have to surrender 8871 first, and we could still work out of the main building.

Lady Francesca, true to herself, was my rock during this process. There was not a lot of help coming my way. I was freaking out because there were so few clubs left, and I had so much equipment that I had no idea what I would do with it. Fortunately, I told the right person about it, and we ended up selling everything to three different people. Francesca and I were in every day, taking things down and apart. It was so surreal; it almost felt out of body at times because it could not be possible. I would look at something and break down.

As much as I resented the lack of help I got from the staff with this, I was still grateful that Francesca was there because she got it, and we had been through it all together for so long. We were always a great team, and even through this experience, we were in tune with one another. We always worked so quickly; we got a lot done in a short time. It was a horrible, horrible experience, tearing apart what took years of love and creativity to create. It was so sad walking in

a room and replaying in your mind all the things that went on inside those four walls, smiling and crying to yourself at the same time.

When people came in to buy the equipment, Robert handled that all for me. It was just too much to see people picking through my stuff and recalling some of the great moments that a particular flogger had experienced or remembered a great spanking session when you picked up a favorite paddle. There was a revisiting of everything for me, and each piece of equipment became very precious and full of sentimental value. I'd just touch it to give it a fond goodbye and "thank you for your service."

Saturday, December 4, 2021, was the last day we were open for sessions. Francesca and I worked the shift together as we promised each other so very long ago that we would do… together until the bitter end. The Ladies made me feel so special that day. Mistress Gloria bought me a cake that said, "Excuse me, your session is ending." These were the words we used to end our sessions with but changed after years of "Knock, Knock" being shouted over the intercom. I had tweaked it to something a little less jolting to the mood. I was very touched by the cake and the thought behind it.

We were busy that day with clients wanting one last session at The Dominion, as we had been for weeks since the announcement. Once the building cleared, hugs were had, promises to keep in touch were shared, tears were shed, and then they were gone. Many had other opportunities, and I knew they would be alright. I felt a lot of

sorrow for the clients who had been coming to us for so long. Where would they go? We were certainly family for so many of them for so many years. Where would they find solace and the listening ears and the understanding they needed? There were other clubs that had emotional attachments to many of the Ladies and to The Dominion itself, but they were hurting, too.

Locking up that day was brutal. It felt empty already, and my heart was broken. I still had time, of course, to spend with Her, but I would be selling her off piece by piece and ripping small pieces of Her heart out daily.

I was grateful to the people who wanted to purchase my equipment. It was all in good shape because it had been loved and taken care of. There were pieces I designed myself that had so many great stories attached to them. Like the metal bondage table I designed for the Vault. I was at a piercing studio in Studio City run by a colorful character called Cliff Cadaver the day I was inspired to have this table. He had this amazing diamond-plate furniture in his lobby and I could see the entire room in my mind. I had a serious metal fetish, so I was easily inspired. He graciously gave me the name of the furniture maker, and I contacted him when I returned home. He was interested and came by to check out the situation.

Well, as fate would have it, he was pretty cute, and the Ladies loved him. I am certain that was a bonus for him. He gave me a quote, and he got to work ASAP. It was a big project, and he was

into it, but the distraction of the Ladies was more than a man could bear. We affectionately called him Metal Boy, and more times than I can remember, I would go by the room, and there would be several ladies in there "helping" him, and he had been stripped down while he was working but was having a ball. I did not care if the work was getting done or not. Thank God, he did not charge me by the hour!

When it was done, it was my pride and joy. The entire room was stainless steel, and the name "The Vault" was very appropriate. That was the piece that hurt the most to lose. I did not want just anyone to have it, and in the end, it found a good home with a very kind man, and I felt okay about it. Watching her get wheeled into the back of a truck was almost more than I could bear.

Francesca gave me all the time she could afford to give me. She dealt with a lot as we were closing, and I appreciated everything she did with me and for me. Emotionally, she was the perfect person to have along with me. We were "slave sisters" and always will be in my eyes. That is a real connection.

Once everyone had picked up (and picked through) my equipment, I invited the Ladies to come and take whatever they wanted that was left. I was amazed at how many showed up and how quickly things disappeared. I think that was actually the worst part for me. None of these people had offered to help Francesca and I, when we needed it most. Some of them didn't even work after COVID, so I felt a little resentful. *( I even heard that some of them*

*had tried to sell the equipment I gave them afterward. How's that for gratitude?)*

The building was empty now. It was hollow, and it echoed the desolation it must have felt being brutalized this way. I felt guilty to do this, but in the end I had no choice.

I still had some time before the sale was final, and I was over there every day, soaking up every memory I possibly could. I cried alone in the building as I walked through Her, and sometimes, I just sat in the emptiness, wondering what was to become of me now. What would become of Her? I knew I would be okay financially, and I had the love of my wonderful husband, but what about not having Lady Hillary or Bunny every day? What would that be like? How would I cope?

The last day I could be there, I walked through, crying alone talking to Her, talking to Lady Laura, apologizing, but I did all I could. I kept my promise to Lady Laura, and I did make her legacy proud. There will never ever be a place as magical and beautiful as The Dominion, and that is just a fact. People will try, but there will be one important missing ingredient: Me!

I opened the front door and closed it behind me one last time. I slowly turned the key in the lock to make this final goodbye last as long as possible. I was sad, but I was proud. The Submissive Bunny who turned The Dominion into the best BDSM club on the planet would always have this memory. And Lady Hillary would always

have her Bunny!

# LOVE NOTES

After we announced our closing, so many love letters were written to The Dominion. I feel it is important to share some of the lovely and heartfelt thoughts of those who called us family and those we helped.

*You were my first session ever, and it's still memorable. You guided me through my BDSM infancy to now, when I still enjoy these activities. I hope there is a bright side to your closing. I also hope there is a bright new chapter in your life. I remember so much from your world that has changed mine.*

**Your friend from Ohio,**
**Lloyd**

*Lady Hillary, I have to thank you for maintaining this magical space where I have felt safe and loved for being my true self, and for that, I am eternally grateful to you.*

**JT**

*I read with sadness your posting that The Dominion was closing. I view most professions as morally positive, neutral, or negative... Yours is truly a moral positive, giving joy to so many who otherwise would have few options to achieve that kind of happiness. I found the people at The Dominion have been universally wonderful.*

### *Dave*

*Your facility holds many fantastic memories for me. Back in the early '90s, I was going through a very dark time in my life, and the kindness of the Ladies literally saved my life... Thank you for the wonderful memories and experiences.*

### *Mark*

*The Dominion allowed me to love and understand my fetish. Thank you so much for being there for me... Thank you, Lady Hillary.*

### *Mike*

*I was so sad to read of your closing. While I was relatively new to The Dominion, that you were there made LA a more welcoming place. Know that you have helped innumerable people, both clients and staff, feel good about themselves and their innate and healthy desires. It's a gift you kept giving. I wish you all the best going forward in your life.*

### *All my love,*
### *Ben*

*I have enjoyed many sessions there and made many friends along the way... I will truly miss being able to play in your fantastic rooms. I wish you all the best in the future. You are truly a legend in the business. Perhaps the place should be declared a historic landmark. I want to say a huge thank you for all you have done for*

*so many of us and, especially your friendship over the years.*

**Jim**

*You have provided me a safe space to explore my kinks when I thought I was alone. Thank you for your kindness and helping me to better understand myself.*

**Josh**

*It saddens me thinking of the days ahead when that sweet Queen Anne building won't know your guiding hand. The rooms will no longer marvel at the fantasies brought to life or sigh with relief when the shackles that gripped our lives begin to fall away even as the play ones do. Then a sense of gladness comes knowing this: after years of constant devotion to others, you're now freeing yourself to accept a life that is simply yours and filled with the things you love.*

**Bill**

*Your announcement closing The Dominion was consistent with the high standards I always experienced at your establishment. After my wife's passing, I enjoyed your place for several decades. You are irreplaceable.*

**Harry**

**Lady Hillary,**

*We so appreciate that you created and maintained a safe and inviting place for people like me to explore my kinky side. I am sad*

*to think The Dominion will be no more, but thankful that it has been there for so long.*

**With gratitude,**
**Tom**

*The Dominion will always live on. You have truly made it a beautiful home and space for me and so many other Ladies, I am proud to have been part of The Dominion family.*

**Barbie**

**Dear Lady Hillary,**

*Thank you for the opportunity to work here. This was the best thing to ever happen to me in my life… this was truly a special place and there will never be another one like it.*

**Mistress Gloria**

*When I first heard The Dominion was closing, I didn't understand why. Was another Lady to fill your shoes? I was sad and confused, and wanted to make sense of the loss. Then I understood you as an artist. I understood the lifetime of passion and dedication to your vision. Your magnum opus. The legacy is best owned by history. I have tremendous respect for that decision. I consider myself very lucky to have received a real BDSM education. Having researched the current landscape for work, I know there will never be another of such caliber. I learned from the best. I have been trained by the women who defined the BDSM culture of the '80s and*

*'90s. Woman owned for 40 years! You and Lady Francesca are icons. Lady Laura must be so proud.*

*I have just begun my BDSM journey and still have so much to learn. Thank you for providing a safe space for me to find myself. I am forever changed and blessed having found my voice and expression. I know I have the strength, courage, boundaries, and language to put my training into practice beyond The Dominion walls. Thank you for this.*

**Clara**

*There'll be no tears of sadness, well, maybe two or ten when I wish to live those days again. But smiles there'll be and laughs and joy just to remember when I felt your hand, your heart and O! The times we shared back then.*

**Bill**

# DOWN THE RABBIT HOLE

A lot of people look forward to retirement. I was not one of that group. If you recall, earlier, I mentioned how much The Dominion balanced me and what a huge difference it made to my life. I went into mourning, and I still mourn the loss of this beautiful place that helped me find my true self and the strength inside of me to keep going. People say when you retire, "Oh, you can find your passion." Well, I had already done that and had lived it for 42 years.

Once the doors were locked, the emptiness set in my heart. I had become accustomed to hopping in my car a few days a week to go hang out with the "kids" and spend some time with Lady Francesca. My entire world had been BDSM, and I never had any other interests to speak of other than my family, who were all grown and gone. There were no other clubs to speak of when I closed, and when some opened, I was just not comfortable there. When one has been The Headmistress for so long, it is hard to let that role go, and I don't think I ever will. I remember how Lady Francesca and I used to laugh about how we would be when we were older and traded in our canes for the real deal, and we could sit on the front porch in our rocking chairs and watch the world pass us by. Well, thankfully, that has not been the case for me. But I don't see a place for me in the community, sadly, and frankly, the community could not care less if I was around or not. It is a shame, but I suspect it is just like life. No

one wants to hear it. It makes me sad. Wisdom and experience are not important when you can learn everything on YouTube or TikTok.

When we were younger, we could go to any BDSM event, and the beauty of it was that anyone and everyone was welcome. We all got along. We did not separate ourselves. We were all just kinky, and that is what mattered. It saddens me to see the separation into tribes.

It is a sad thing to admit that I would feel uncomfortable anywhere I went to play. Part of it is my age, and the other is that a lot of people just don't like me. That is my perception. I was always one of those people who gave myself more credit than I should have for being loved. My husband calls it "cupboard love." I don't have a cupboard now, so everyone is gone. I have nothing to offer them anymore. I have a few Old-School friends, and of course, Lady Francesca is still in my life. I suspect my expectations, once again, are unrealistic. One thing Lady Laura had was Bunny. I could use a Bunny about now.

I was so lucky to grow up in the scene when I did because, for all its flaws, it was amazing and real. It was not just a way to earn a quick buck; it was a calling, and you were either good or you were gone. We were a community of Musketeers.

I don't know what the future holds for me. I have lost my balance, and I struggle to find it. I have debilitating anxiety and

depression, which keeps me from doing much. This really sucks because I can go anywhere I wish and pretty much do anything I like.

One day, my Bunny will come out again and help me find my strength, and I will find happiness some other way. Losing The Dominion was not a positive thing for me, but it was a necessary one.

Still, I am optimistic. Perhaps I will play the piano at Carnegie Hall one day. I will travel to Europe and make new memories for us and relive some old ones.

The days have been long and a lot of them lonely since I closed The Dominion. I have always won my battles, and I plan on winning this one, too. The Dominion will always be a part of me, and I know there will never be another club that comes close to the reputation and beauty The Dominion held for those who were lucky enough to know Her.

I was blessed with the life of The Dominion, and all of its history and memories will be mine to hold forever. I know a lot of people have varying opinions of kink, and a lot of outsiders judge us mercilessly but don't even know us, which is very much the case for anything outside of their norms. I encourage people to have the courage to do what is in their hearts. Were it not for BDSM, my life would have been vastly different, and I probably would not have survived past 40. My heart and soul were filled with love from Kink.

It gave me life, and I hope I made it a better place while I was relevant. No one could have loved kink more. I gave our Dominion my best and She gave me all her love and wonder and excitement. I met so many wonderful men whom I deeply respected and developed great kinships with. Thousands of amazing women passed through The Dominion in the years I was there, and they all took a piece of Her and threw it out to the universe in one way or another when they left.

I wish the tolerance that existed when I began my journey still existed. Sadly, it has lost some of its soul with all the changes it has had to endure over the years. When the money becomes more important than the kink, it weakens the whole point of it slowly and painfully. I feel so blessed to have been there and lived through the Old Guard, and I feel sadness for those who will never experience the glory days of BDSM and the pride one feels after a job well done.

I am so grateful and honored to have had the trust of the friends who kept us going all those years. I know The Dominion will remain in their hearts as well. The Dominion touched a lot of lives and made a difference to so many people. She gave them courage and permission to be themselves and share their secrets with her, and they are now locked inside her, safe and sound!

I will be alright. There won't be a day I don't think of The Dominion or a day I don't count the blessings She afforded me. The biggest blessing she gave me is my Sir Robert. He never gives up

288

on me, and he loves me no matter what. I have more blessings than most, and the biggest one is my husband, who loves me unconditionally and spends his life trying to make me happy. That's it, my purpose. Spending the rest of my life with the best guy on the planet who would do anything to make me happy. So many people would give anything to be as lucky as I am, and I'm grateful.

# CLOSING THOUGHTS

As I close this book, I want to thank you for taking the time to listen to and hopefully learn from my story. Before we part, I'd like to leave you with the closing message I posted on The Dominion's website near the end of 2021, as I think it's still fitting to this day.

***Dear Dominion Friends,***

*As I close this chapter of my life, I am filled with so many emotions and beautiful memories. Forty years is a long time, and I have grown and learned so much. Like many Ladies who passed through this place, The Dominion changed me and my life. Like many of you, I was searching for somewhere I would be understood and not made to feel "less than."*

*The Dominion provided a safe space for me to grow and learn to accept myself as the person I was and to take away the stigma of being "different" in a world that prefers cookie-cutter perfection.*

*I had the great privilege to work with Lady Laura, the first woman to own a dungeon in Los Angeles. Lady Laura was my mentor, Mother, Mistress, and friend. She was a trailblazer in the community, a true Diva and inspiration.*

*This has not always been an easy journey. There were lots of obstacles to cross to keep the place going, including fighting City*

*Hall and male competitors who did not feel a woman had the right to run a dungeon. Boy, were they wrong!*

*One of the great moments in Los Angeles's BDSM history was the day that all BDSM clubs were owned by women, and "Sisters were doin' it for themselves!" The '80s and '90s were pretty exploitative for women in the houses, and we were able to change that, which I am very proud of.*

*I have much to be proud of. I tried to instill in the women who passed through here a sense of pride in who they were and teach them they were in charge, no matter what their position and the most important thing was that NO MEANS NO!*

*The Dominion was a Sisterhood, and that was part of the success story. The other part of the success was caring for our friends who came to visit. There are so many fond memories of people who have been with us from the beginning of The Dominion to the precious "newbies" we are meeting in our last days. The Dominion gave me self-esteem and I became proud of who I was and valued my kinks and differences as a bonus.*

*I was a single mother of three, and The Dominion afforded me the luxury of making a living sufficient to take care of my children completely on my own.*

*I love being a Dungeon Mother. I think I will miss this the most.*

*I have so many people to thank.*

I thank all of the Ladies who had my back and tried their hardest to keep this place going and have stuck with me until the bittersweet end.

I thank our Dominion friends who kept coming back and sharing their fantasies with us.

I thank my husband, who I met here, for his constant support and love. The Dominion and I have been a lot of work, and he rose to the occasion!

What can I say about my dearest friend in the world? Lady Francesca, who has been with me through so much and has stuck with me through the best and worst of times. I have always said I could not have done it without her, and that is just a fact. She is my chosen Sister and my best friend, and I love her dearly. We did it together and will remain friends for life.

There is so much to say… too many stories, too many good times and bad, and there is just no way I can express to all of you what this journey has meant for me.

The Dominion has been a blessing to me, and I am confident I did Lady Laura proud. There will never be another place like The Dominion with a Sisterhood like we had. We have learned and grown so much together.

I am filled with pride and gratitude as we close the doors, and I know you will think of us on occasion and smile. I know I will once

*I get past the tears.*

*I have loved you all.*

**Lady Hillary,**
**Headmistress of The Dominion.**

www.ingramcontent.com/pod-product-compliance
Lightning Source LLC
Chambersburg PA
CBHW051507120626
46551CB00012B/815